THE GREAT PAWN HUNTER CHESS TUTORIAL

Stories, Poetry and Games

Manus Patrick Fealy

Bloomington, IN   authorHOUSE   Milton Keynes, UK

AuthorHouse™
1663 Liberty Drive, Suite 200
Bloomington, IN 47403
www.authorhouse.com
Phone: 1-800-839-8640

AuthorHouse™ UK Ltd.
500 Avebury Boulevard
Central Milton Keynes, MK9 2BE
www.authorhouse.co.uk
Phone: 08001974150

© 2006 Manus Patrick Fealy. All rights reserved.

No part of this book may be reproduced, stored in a retrieval system, or transmitted by any means without the written permission of the author.

First published by AuthorHouse 6/5/2006

ISBN: 1-4259-4081-1 (sc)

Library of Congress Control Number: 2006905038

Printed in the United States of America
Bloomington, Indiana

This book is printed on acid-free paper.

CONTENTS

INTRODUCTION.................................. 4

The Stories:

THE ROOK.................................... 7

THE KNIGHT 11

THE BISHOP 17

THE QUEEN 22

THE KING 28

THE PAWN.................................. 33

THE FIRST CHESS TOURNAMENT...... 39

GOING TO A CHESS CLUB 46

THE INITIATIVE 51

THE MOUSE'S PLAN 56

A BETTER MOVE 61

THE BARTENDER 66

FREE AT LAST 74

THE CLEVER FOX 79

FRIED LIVER 83

BROTHERLY LOVE 93

A KNIGHT'S MOVES 99

STANDING GROUND 106

BUGOLOGY, THE GREAT ESCAPE 114

ZUGZWANG 118

HARMONY 126

BATTLE ON THE MOUNTAIN 132

THE INTREPID WARRIOR 141

THE WISDOM OF SOLOMON 152

A TEACUP FULL OF STEAM 162

ELUSIVE AND FREE 170

THE RUSTY OLD GATE	**179**
THE IGLOO HAS LANDED	**191**
BITS AND BYTES	**201**
THE HUMMING BIRD	**210**
COMING HOME	**221**
PEBBLES	**230**
THE PURSUIT OF HAPPINESS	**240**
WHERE RAINBOWS ARCH	**251**
DOWNWIND FROM CHECKMATE	**261**
A LITTLE WEE WHISKEY	**274**
RICKETY TICKITY TOCK	**284**
TRIALS AND TRIBULATIONS	**295**

Appendixes

Openings	302
Players	303
Poems	304, 305
Index	306, 307

Introduction

I was born of Irish immigrant parents. My mother was from Donegal and my father was from County Kerry Ireland. They met here in Boston at Hibernian Hall in Roxbury. My Dad worked as a common laborer and my mother worked as a housekeeper to make ends meet. They stayed married together through all the ups and downs for all of their lives.

I grew up playing on the streets of Boston where I was constantly getting in fights. Many of the things that the characters in my stories do are gained from the experiences of my childhood here in the neighborhoods. One day, I asked the librarians in my community if I could offer a chess program for the children and I have been teaching chess ever since.

When I first started writing my stories, they were only to entertain my father and me. Since, after my mother's death we were a bit lonely. I would publish my stories, poetry and lessons on the internet for the fun of it. After my father died, I wrote the stories mainly for the good people in cyberspace. I gained a following from chess players in many countries and it is for all of you that I write.

I feel very blessed to have family and friends that have stayed with me through the ups and downs. I hope that this little book brings a smile to each reader who takes the chance and opens its covers.

The Great Pawn Hunter
Manny Paddy Fealy
May 15, 2006

Never No More To Weep
A poem

Never cry lying down love.
The tears go in your ears.
Sit up straight and settle down
and I'll wipe away your fears.

Friend, what should please
the Highest One?
Not gold or jewels, they
could never lend
a helping hand
to wipe a tear away.

And, in giving, there's receiving.
Please believe me when I say:
"God knows every nook and cranny
of every soul who's ever prayed."

And, a single drop of His mercy
would forgive the sins of man,
but He chooses to, act through you.
So pray love, if you can.

And, in acting there's reacting.
A ripple to the farthest shore
can start from a single tear drop.
So, cry my love no more.

And, in seeing, there's believing
a birth conceiving of this thought:
God gave His only Son for us.
With His Passion, we were bought.

And from the tide there was a ripple,
started far across the sea,
in the little town of Nazareth
in the land of Galilee.

And, He brings
the brave and the mighty
and the lowly
to bended knee.
For there is only One,
One and only.
True and just,
is He
who can wipe away
our teardrops
for all eternity.
And, He asks only love and mercy
from His dear humanity.

So, dry your ears and wipe your eyes.
Rest peaceful as you sleep.
I pray to God
watch over you.
In His heart
your soul to keep.

Ever ever, dear love, forever
And never no more
to weep.

The Great Pawn Hunter

The Rook

Old Maestro walked the country road, past the town and down to the brook. It had rained the night before and the brook was filled to its banks. He slowed, looked up at the sky, and at the trees green with leaves and at the nests filled with life ...life that had yet to see the break of day and he sighed...

It was early morning. The Great Pawn Hunter and The Restless Knight were sitting by the brook and had their feet in the water. The chess players could see Old Maestro coming near with his cup in one hand and pushing a carriage in the other. The carriage was filled with empty bottles that Old Maestro collected and exchanged for five cents a bottle at the store. He was not a greedy man. He earned enough to get him through life, no more no less. Old Maestro's feet were sore from his morning walk. He came over to the chess players, sat down near them, and dipped his feet into the water. The chess players were eager to ask Old Maestro a question. "Old Maestro," said The Great Pawn Hunter, "how do you play chess?" Old Maestro smiled and motioned with his feet in the water. He wiggled his toes left and he wiggled his toes right, up and down, diagonally, and finally in a circle. The Great Pawn Hunter and The Restless Knight didn't know that Old Maestro was tracing the paths of the pieces with his feet in the water. "I'll tell you how I play," he said, "but, we must start at the beginning." The Restless Knight pulled out her pocket chess board for the old man...

The Great Pawn Hunter - 8

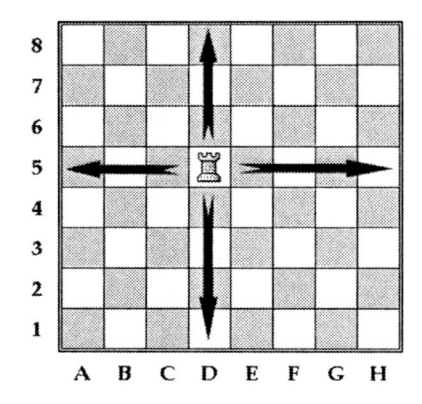

Old Maestro said to them "Listen and I will tell you my secret." The chess players stared intently at the pocket chess board. He whispered to them..."The pieces," he said, "have invisible shapes! The rook," he said, "must travel in a straight line and cannot hop over other pieces. This anyone can tell you. However, the invisible shape of the rook is seen by the paths that it can travel. If you place a pebble on every square that the rook can move to you will find its hidden shape." The Great Pawn Hunter did as Old Maestro asked and discovered the hidden shape is a 'cross'. In this case, the rook, sitting on the d5 square, can move to any square in the path from (a5 to h5). It can also move to any square from (d1 to d8).

"Do you want to hear more?" asked Old Maestro. The chess players shouted "Yes!" with anticipation. "The value of a rook," said Old Maestro, "is worth five points and you must try not to trade it for a lesser valued piece unless you have something to gain like checkmate!" This the chess players knew already. "Here," he said "is a secret: If the rook sits on the back row behind a bunch of pawns or pieces then it does not have its full shape of a 'cross' because the other pieces get in its way!" This the chess players didn't know. "So, this means it is not worth the five points. You are playing without a rook! You must bring it out into the open, like a champion, so that it can be what it aspires to be...a cross."

The chess players received a valuable lesson. but their attention spans had reached their limits. They agreed to meet the next day. However, before they left, the chess players dug down deep into their bubble gum money and dropped some change into Old Maestro's cup.

The Rook
A poem

I learned from Old Maestro
about a rook.
Five points in a castle,
a lesson I took.
Its shape is a 'cross'
when out on a file.
Now I'm hooked
and I've got style.
So, take this weapon
and make it work.
Please, don't laugh
and please don't smirk.
For a rook is dangerous,
it covers all squares.
I'd rather fight lions,
tigers and bears!!!

The Great Pawn Hunter

The Knight

Gradually the bubble grew...larger, larger, cheeks straining, jaws hurting, till it was as large as The Great Pawn Hunters face. Then, as if it were a sign, a gift of relief, the bubble popped and he knew he had set a house record. Could anyone blow one grander?...not on this planet...or so he thought. The Great Pawn Hunter got on his bicycle and peddled over to The Restless Knight's house. He still had bubble gum on his nose and chin...all in all, a very successful bubble. He was smiling as he rang The Restless Knight's doorbell.

Now, on this day, The Restless Knight was busy, running around in her feet, looking for something. She went through all her shirts, jeans, and jacket but to no avail. She could not find the pack of bubble gum she was looking for. Her mother said "Restless, did you look under your bed." However, Restless replied "Mom why would it be under my bed." Her mother replied "Well you've looked everywhere else." Ahhh, the process of elimination, the reasoning behind all scientific, logical, non-bubble blowing thought...and, an adult's answer for everything. Restless looked under the bed but all she could find were her shoes, an empty bubble gum wrapper, and a pawn. Ah, a clue! "The Great Pawn Hunter must have eaten it," said Restless. "Well, put on your shoes and we will go to the store." said her mother. Restless went to put on her shoes and what fell out but her pack of "Bigger Bubble" bubble gum, a God send, just what she was looking for. She felt guilty for thinking such bad things about The Great Pawn Hunter. But, all that was left, in the pack of bubble gum, were empty bubble gum wrappers and a half eaten stick of gum...only enough to practice with. "Can we pick up a pack of gum at the store?" asked Restless. "Okay," said her mother "if it will make you happy."

On the way to the store they passed Old Maestro. Restless knew that it would take him some time to reach their street collecting bottles. They waved and beeped the horn as they drove by. Now, after they arrived at the store, Restless ran to the candy isle and started looking for her brand of gum "Bigger Bubble" the brand that astronauts chew. But she couldn't find it. That was her favorite gum. She would have to settle for a brand unknown to her. "Well, how about this one?" said her mother. "That's chewing gum," said Restless, "not bubble gum." Adults...go figure. Finally, she picked a brand hoping for the best.

She arrived home with her mother to see The Great Pawn Hunter sitting on her porch extracting something from his hair. It was the remnants of another successful bubble. His smile was glowing from ear to ear and so was the bubble gum. They ran into the house, through the hallway and into the kitchen. This was the place where so many contests were held in the past. Yes, held in this perfect place were the pie eating contest, the house of cards contest, and now coming to a kitchen near you ...a bubble blowing contest.

Well, The Great Pawn Hunter took out a piece of "Bigger Bubble" bubble gum and started chewing. "You stole that bubble gum," said Restless. "I did not," said The Great Pawn Hunter, "I acquired it."

However, the look on his face could not be described as The Restless Knight produced her fresh pack of "Ultra Bubble,(new and improved)" bubble gum. "Want a piece?" asked Restless. The Great Pawn Hunter said "No thanks, your old brand will do just fine." He was very confident. The chess players chewed and chewed. Even though Ultra Bubble was clearly the better bubble gum, The Great Pawn Hunter had more experience with Bigger Bubble, in effect, canceling each other out. The chess players were still chewing as Old Maestro rang the doorbell.

Old Maestro entered into the kitchen and saw the two chess players in a heated contest with bubbles growing out of their faces as if they were blimps. He sensed the tension between the two. "Can I have a piece?" asked Old Maestro. The chess players didn't know that Old Maestro chewed gum. After all, he only had three teeth left in his mouth. But, somehow he managed. He blew his first bubble, and it was...a small one. "Sorry Old Maestro," said The Great Pawn Hunter "we have already blown bigger bubbles than that." But Old Maestro was not finished. He motioned with his hand as if to say: "Wait a minute" and produced something grand, something that would deflate the tension and raise the bubble blowing contest to a new level...a bubble within a bubble. They cheered and applauded and they forgot what they were fighting about. For, they both wanted to learn how to do it. Yes, Old Maestro was a true master. Now they had a common goal set by a great diplomat, but some things are meant to be kept secret and revealed another day. For now though, it was time for a chess lesson. They set up the chess board:

The Great Pawn Hunter - 14

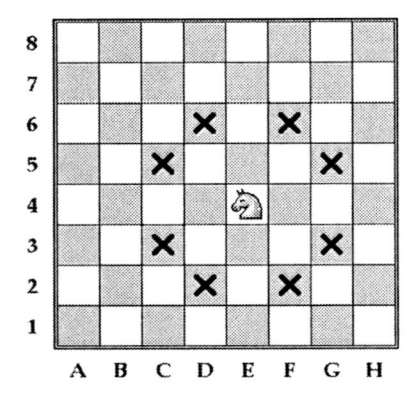

"A knight," said Old Maestro, "moves like the letter 'L'." If you look at the knight upside down it is shaped like the letter 'L' too. However, if you put a pebble on all the squares that the knight can move to you will find its hidden shape." The chess players did this and found that the knight was really a 'circle'.

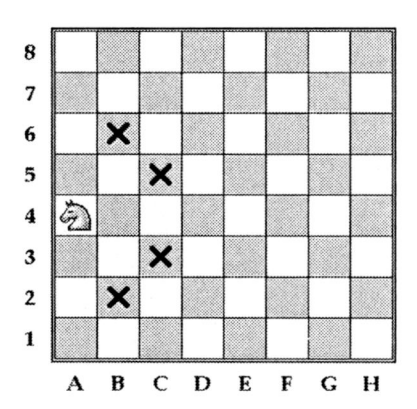

"Place the knight on the side of the board", asked Old Maestro. The chess players did and discovered that on the side of the board the knight is only half of a circle.

The Great Pawn Hunter - 15

Old Maestro asked them "So, what would you rather have...a full circle or half a circle?" The chess players replied, "A full circle." Old Maestro asked them "Where do you get the full circle?" They replied, "In the center." "Yes,", said Old Maestro, "and that is why we should attack the center...so our pieces can have full shape."

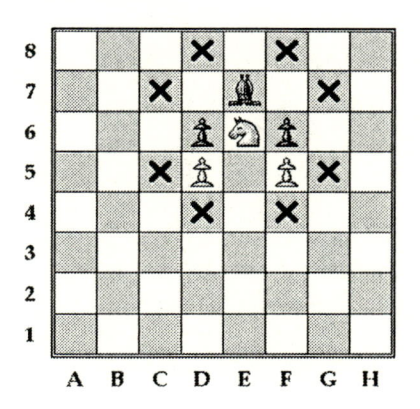

Old Maestro said "Knights are allowed to hop over other pieces, but here is a secret: knights are better than the bishops when the center is closed and locked up with pawns" and he showed them an example. "On the board," he said "the knight can jump over all the pawns and can travel free. However, the bishop is controlled by the knight. It cannot move because the pawns block its escape and the knight controls the (d8) and (f8) squares."

Well, the chess lesson was over but not before The Great Pawn Hunter had seen the error of his ways and offered Restless the rest of her bubble gum.

Common Ground
A poem

Many times we make mistakes,
some people give,
some people take.
Here is some wisdom
from the lost and found:
Set a new goal
where there's common ground.
Now, mind you, there will be
give and take,
but just remember
what is at stake.
If all it takes is blowing a bubble
It's such a small price
to stay out of trouble.

The Great Pawn Hunter

The Bishop

The Restless Knight awoke. She had dreamed of flowers, chocolates and chess. Her mother was in the kitchen making a meal. "Restless," came a shout from the kitchen, "breakfast is ready," said her mother. "I'll be right down mom," shouted The Restless Knight from her bedroom. Restless put on her favorite clothes: jeans, sneakers, and her favorite shirt with a knight on the pocket. "Mom, I don't have time to eat. I have to go meet Old Maestro for a chess lesson," said Restless. This was the last thing her mother wanted to hear, after spending the time to make the meal. However, her mother gave this some thought. "Maybe," she thought, "it would be good for Restless to fast a day...It would save on the dishes." However, then the guilt set in. "Restless, please eat your breakfast," said her mother. Now, her mother knew that Old Maestro lived from day to day, but her mother also knew there was no place safer than being with Old Maestro. "By the way," she said, "give this to Old Maestro when you meet him." She handed her a bag full of pancakes. This was his favorite thing to eat. "Thanks mom," said Restless and they both smiled.

Little did they know that The Great Pawn Hunter was busy rushing out the door, at this very moment, without a bite in his stomach and his stomach was grumbling. He made it over to The Restless Knight's house, jumped off of his bicycle, and ran up the steps of the porch to her door. Ring went the doorbell. "That's The Great Pawn Hunter, mom," said Restless, and she moved to get up from the kitchen table. "Stay right there and finish your meal," said her mother, "I'll answer it." Her mother opened the door. However, before her mother could answer he said "Are those your award winning pancakes I smell." The Restless Knight heard him from the kitchen. She knew The Great Pawn Hunter could charm the pancakes out of any cook...she wolfed down the rest of her meal. Meanwhile, at the door, her mother smiled, to buy some time, but in the long run...she didn't stand a chance. "Come on in," she said, "and have a bite to eat."

Well, the meal disappeared in a gulp and a grumble and The Great Pawn Hunter was quick to compliment her mother on what a fine cook she was. But, the minutes were ticking by and they knew they had to get over to meet Old Maestro for the chess lesson. They took the meal for Old Maestro, ran out the door, got on their bicycles and quickly peddled down the street and disappeared out of sight.

They arrived as Old Maestro was sitting down on the picnic bench by the brook. This time he had brought his chessboard and pieces. The chess players set the pieces up for him and they began to talk. "What is the bishop?" asked The Restless Knight. Old Maestro replied "The bishop travels diagonally. It can not jump over other pieces if they are in its way. If you place it on the square (e4) and place a pebble where it can move to you will discover its hidden shape." The Restless Knight did as he asked and discovered the bishop was really an "X" covering a total of fourteen squares.

The Great Pawn Hunter - 19

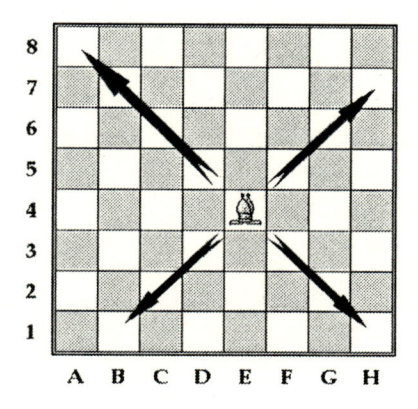

"Now, put the bishop on the side of the board," asked Old Maestro. She did as he asked. Old Maestro asked "Now put a pebble on the bishop's paths and you will discover something." She did and she discovered that on the side of the board the bishop was only half an "X" covering a total of only eight squares.

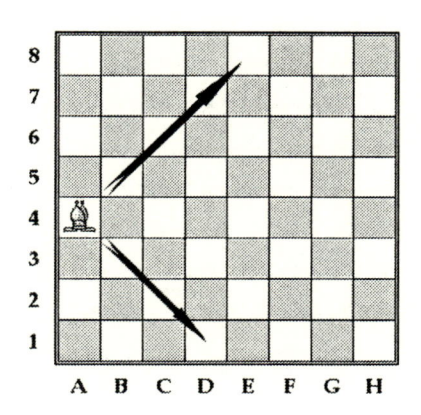

"What does this mean to me as a player?" asked Restless. Old Maestro said "What would you rather have...a full 'X' or half of an 'X'?" She said a full

'X'...Old Maestro said "That's correct. On what part of the board do you get the full 'X'?". She said "In the center." Old Maestro smiled...he knew he had got his idea across to her. "Yes," he said, "and that is why you must attack the center ...so your pieces will have what?"...and The Great Pawn Hunter shouted "Full Shape!"

"When you start out the game with two bishops," said Old Maestro, "One bishop sits on a dark square. It must always travel on the dark squares. Another bishop sits on a light square. It must always stay on the light squares". He whispered again, listen and I will tell you a secret: If a dark squared bishop is lost for your opponent, then your opponent loses three points and becomes weak on the dark squares. Use your dark squared bishop to attack on those squares." The Restless Knight replied "So, the same must be true for the light squared bishop."...and she was right again. Well, the lesson was over and they agreed to meet again the following day, but not before they gave Old Maestro the pancakes that The Restless Knight's mother had made.

The Bishop
A poem

The Bishop is a wonderful piece.
It moves to the west.
It moves to the east.
It travels by angles.
Its points measure three
And, when you place it,
in the center,
an 'X' it will be.

The Great Pawn Hunter

The Queen

To every uneventful day there is that anticipation to when excitement and laughter will flow like a bubbling brook. Hopefully, that moment would arrive, at about 2:00 pm, when Old Maestro would make his way down the street collecting bottles...and talk about The Great Pawn Hunter's favorite subject...chess. This one old man with tattered clothes and eyes that shone like steel could lift one's spirits and make one laugh if only for a moment...a rare breed. A horse that couldn't be broken...

On this day, The Great Pawn Hunter was called out like a gun fighter in the streets. His father needed him to hold a piece of wood, fixed in place, while he cut it with an electric saw. The demand was issued..."Come out and hold a piece of wood for me," shouted his father. The Great Pawn Hunter dropped what he was doing. He packed a screwdriver, a hammer, and a chisel into his work belt. A crowbar was an added touch that hung real low and scraped across the floor, like a shotgun, as he ran out of the house. "Draw a line on the wood and mark an 'X' on the piece to be cut off," said his father. The Great Pawn Hunter whistled as if there were a bullet rushing by. It was a near miss. "Now, hold the wood for me," said his father. The Great Pawn Hunter sensed his father's itchy trigger finger. It was only a matter of time. He put his hand onto the wood and covered the pencil mark with his hands. "But, whatever you do," said his father "don't"...It was too late. The Great Pawn Hunter had covered the pencil lines with his hands. But the bullet, that was shot, turned into rubber when his father said "No son, that is not the way. You must never cover the pencil marks...that is where the saw blade runs." The Great Pawn Hunter smiled and said "Oops." Well, he put his hands the right way onto the wood, held it firm, and his father began to cut. However, the saw hissed and burred and smoke began to come out from between the plank he was cutting. But his father kept on cutting. They looked at the burn marks on the edge of the wood and then at each other in a confused sort of way. They had an inkling that something was wrong but they didn't know what. His father said "Don't worry...I know what I am doing." as if The Great Pawn Hunter had never heard that one before. It was a miracle that any wood was cut at all. You see, the saw blade had been put in backwards. When they finally found out, they had already cut the plank lengthways. The Great Pawn Hunter saw his opportunity and shot from the hips, "Well, Dad, we could always use it for kindling!" His father smiled and turned a lovely shade of red...mortally wounded.

Well, The Restless Knight had met Old Maestro at the top of the street and they were making their way down to The Great Pawn Hunter's house. They were wondering where all the smoke was coming from. "Quick Dad," said The Great Pawn Hunter, "change the saw blade before The Restless Knight gets here...or we will never hear the end of it." Now there was a new gunfighter in town, The Restless Knight, and she was quick on the draw too. His father quickly scrambled to find a wrench to take the saw blade off, but it was too late. Old Maestro and Restless were in sight. "Son, hide this saw and give me the handsaw from the bucket." Well, The Great Pawn Hunter quickly gave him the handsaw and hid the electric saw in the bushes.

"Hi everyone, what ya up to," said Restless. "Oh, nothing much," said the father and son at the same time. The Great Pawn Hunter decided to decoy The Restless Knight before she had the chance to ask about the saw. "Restless, would you like a glass of lemonade. We can get it in the house," said he. Restless, knew there was something up. She could smell it and it smelled like burnt wood! "No thanks, maybe later," said she. "How did you cut the wood?" asked The Restless Knight. Her gun went off...KABANG! The Great Pawn Hunter's father produced the handsaw. "With this," he said. However, his shot was wide and missed The Restless Knight completely. For, you see, the handsaw was only one foot in length counting the handle and things didn't add up. The plank was much too long to be cut with a small handsaw.

The Restless Knight got very suspicious and wanted to get to the root of the problem. "You cut that long plank with that one foot saw," said Restless, "How did you do it?" KABANG! Her gun went off again. "With hard work and sweat," said The Great Pawn Hunter. He was trying to cover up but the guilt shown up on his face. He was slightly wounded but you never cry over the fleshy stuff.

Old Maestro sensed their desperation. "It is time for a chess lesson, isn't it," said he. Finally, the Marshal had arrived! The Great Pawn Hunter quickly said "Yes, let's get the chess set Restless"...and all three went into the house...a narrow escape! Now, once the chessboard had been set up, Old Maestro began to teach. "The Queen", he said, "moves in a straight line. If you place the queen in the middle of the board on the (e4) square and then place a pebble on every square that the queen can move to, you will find its invisible shape. The players did this and found that the queen was a 'star.'

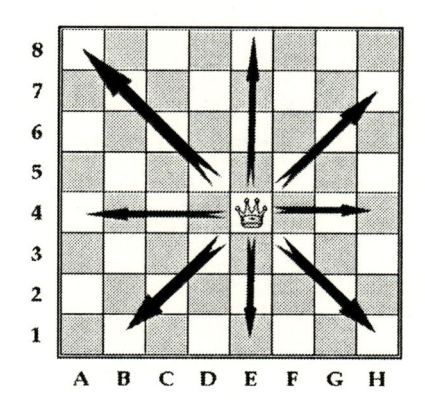

"The queen," said Old Maestro, "travels like a rook's cross and like a bishop's 'X', these two pieces combine to form the queen. It cannot hop over other pieces and must travel in a straight line," said he. "She is the most powerful piece on the board and is worth 9 points. Try never to trade her for a lower valued piece unless you can gain something that is worth more than 9 points...like checkmate, but here is a secret," said he, and the chess players listened attentively, "Most of the time, you must attack with a lesser valued piece first so that the queen can enter into the action last. Then she will control the game. However, if she attacks first, she can be traded off and there goes your 9 points."

Now when the lesson was over, the chess players left the house and The Restless Knight looked over the porch. She could see something funny in the bushes. She walked down the steps and over to the object. It was the electric saw with the saw blade reversed. "Hard work and sweat...Hmmmm," thought Restless. She had finally got to the root of it all. However, she didn't want to embarrass them. She paused only for a moment and then passed it by without a remark...and The Great Pawn Hunter waved her goodbye with a face as red as could be...mortally wounded...like father like son. They remained the best of friends.

The Queen
A poem

The Queen is very powerful.
Nine points in all is she.
Her path is like a star
and she's as beautiful as can be.
She covers all the squares
and if you pay attention,
she will treat you like a king
and mistakes we won't mention.

The Great Pawn Hunter

The King

It was a blustery afternoon in the shadow of a cold wintry day. Slowly The Great Pawn Hunter climbed, up between the two adjacent buildings, with his arms and legs outstretched. Each limb was pressing against the cold brick walls. First he placed the legs, to get a grip, and then the hands, constantly moving upwards, each limb helping the other...

He climbed past the first window where his neighbor, Mrs. Nosybottoms, lived. She was constantly on the alert, ever vigil for any sign of life in the neighborhood. Of course, most days, there wasn't any mischief. However, she would be the first with the story if there was. Fortunately, for The Great Pawn Hunter, it was her nap time and he could climb in peace. He made it past the first floor window. The shades were drawn. He was in luck. From this height, he could see across the street. But that wasn't good enough. He wanted to see his perfect place...the tree on the hill. But, for that mighty cause, he would have to climb higher and, for that great goal, climb he did...

This was not his first time climbing. He had climbed Trapper's wall that stretched down the length of his street. The bullies in the neighborhood used to hide behind it in wait for any person, unlucky enough, to walk beside it. The bullies would jump out from behind it and pounce on the unsuspecting bystander until he said "UNCLE" ...and that unsuspecting bystander was...The Great Pawn Hunter.
Now, The Great Pawn Hunter was not the kind to be pushed around. Even though he lacked the size to

contend with them, he refused to cross to the other side of the street. "It's the principle of the thing," he said. And as a result, he was pounced upon, day after day, until he could spell "UNCLE" backwards, forwards, sideways, and upside down.

But, this all came to an end one day when his new neighbor, The Restless Knight, saw him in distress and came running. What she lacked in size, she more than made up in pure ferocity. She grabbed the biggest bully by the belly button pushed him down and sat on him until he could spell..."butterfly," "cupcake," "lily,", and "checkmate!" These were all of her favorite things and friendship soon grew between the two chess players. It is a funny thing, what you think about, when you are climbing...

The Great Pawn Hunter had made it up to the second floor. He could see the delicatessen. His father used to give him money to get German bologna there. This was his favorite food to eat and it was an adventure too when he was younger. The first time he was allowed to go out on his own, his father had asked him to go to the deli because:
Number one: He wouldn't have to cross the street.
Number two: Unbeknownst to The Great Pawn Hunter, the butcher would call if there was a problem.
Number three: The father loved German Bologna!
The Great Pawn Hunter's belly started to grumble. He would have to go home soon to get something to eat. But he had not attained his goal yet. He climbed higher. When he got to the third floor he stopped. His hands and feet were getting tired. He looked around and could see something off in the distance. It was small but with concentration he

could make it out...it was the great tree on the hill. He sighed. He had reached his goal.

Going down, though, was not as easy as going up. He made it down to the second floor. However, the way he went down was not the way he went up. The wind had pushed him sideways brick by brick...a little bit at a time. As he climbed down past the second floor, he went to place his foot below him and found he had drifted over Mrs. Nosybottoms window. "Oh, Nuts!" said he. Mrs. Nosybottoms came to look out. She looked downward, left, and then right, everywhere but up. His limbs were getting exhausted. His palms were sweating and his knees were starting to buckle. She turned around, to walk away, and his legs gave out. Quickly he dropped past the window and landed on the snow below him. Nothing was hurt but his pride. But Mrs. Nosybottoms came back out to see him lying on his back. "Get up from there," she said "or you'll catch your death of cold." He pretended to make an angel in the snow. She smiled and walked back into the kitchen...another narrow escape!

The Great Pawn Hunter - 31

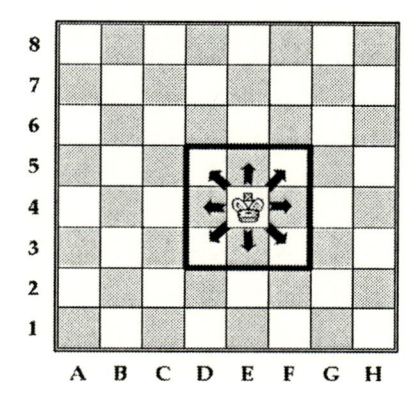

He made it to his favorite place on earth for his chess lesson with Old Maestro...the great tree on the hill. Today Old Maestro would teach him about the King. "The King," said Old Maestro, "can only move one square in every direction. If you place a pebble on every square that the king can move to you will find its invisible shape." The chess players did this and found that the King was a 'square'..."or a very small 'star'," said The Restless Knight.

"Here is a secret," said Old Maestro "The King must come out from its corner to the center of the board to be what he wants to be...a square! But at the beginning of the game there are too many pieces on the board and he can be captured. So, it is best for him go there after most of the pieces, like the rooks and the queens, come off the board. It is then that he can escort pawns to the queening square and shine like a champion!"

Well, the chess lesson was over and the chess players agreed to meet another day. Yes, another day...filled with possibilities.

The King
A poem

The King, the object of the game
is not so square you see.
He shines just like a star.
Although, a small one he must be,
but, later in the game,
he comes out with all his cares
and escorts the lowly pawns
to the queening squares.
So, if you want to play
be the king, you see,
and not another wood pusher
that moves from A to B.

The Great Pawn Hunter

The Pawn

It was another day at school. The clouds were not so bright. The sky was not so blue. But, today was a day unlike any other. For you see, it was The Great Pawn Hunter's birthday. The lights in the classroom were turned out and the cake was brought in. The flicker of the candles shone bright in the chess players eyes. Everyone had a piece of the cake...everyone except the mouse who was left alone, unnoticed in the corner of the room...and this is where our story begins...

The Great Pawn Hunter opened up his present. It looked as though it could be a telescope, but it was something even better: a rollup tournament chess mat and the pieces to boot. When The Talker saw this, his eyes almost burst out of his head with envy. He said, "Nice chess mat, make sure someone doesn't steal it," in a menacing sort of way. The Great Pawn Hunter had to be excused. The Talker had made him so nervous he had to go to the bathroom. When he came back and placed his pieces on the chess mat, all were there except one unlucky pawn, gone missing, and a note. It read:

**Deliver a pound of cheese
to the great tree on the hill,
by twelve midnight,
before
the little pawn gets it!**

How could The Talker be so cruel to play such a terrible joke on The Great Pawn Hunter. He had a piece of birthday cake...wasn't that enough?

The Great Pawn Hunter - 34

"Talker," said The Great Pawn Hunter "Did you see my pawn? It's gone missing." "You should take better care of your pieces," said The Talker, "I didn't take it," said he with a smile on his face. Well, if The Talker didn't take it, the smile on his face said...he knew who did!

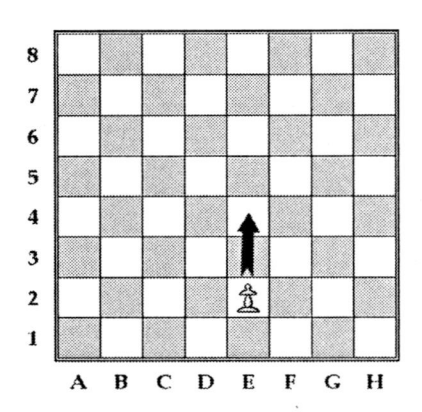

Now, The Great Pawn Hunter went to his chess lesson and Old Maestro taught him about pawns. "Pawns," said Old Maestro "are said to be the soul of chess. The pawns form a skeleton that all the pieces have to play around. Once a pawn moves forward or captures, it can never retreat. So be very cautious when moving them. On its first move, a pawn can move two squares. After that, the same pawn can only move one square at a time."

The Great Pawn Hunter - 35

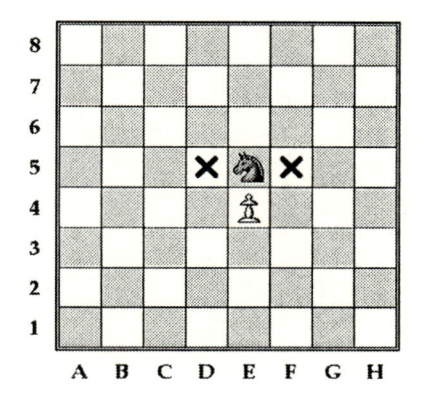

Old Maestro said "A pawn can only move forward but it captures diagonally. If a pawn was on the square (e4) then it can capture any enemy piece that sits on the (d5) or (f5) squares. It cannot capture a piece that is directly in front of it and for that reason the square in front of your pawn can become weak. It is an ideal place for your opponent to camp his pieces."

Old Maestro said "Here is a secret: control the square in front of your pawn with your other pieces. This will help guide the pawn all the way up the file to the queening square. When the pawn gets to the other end it can become a queen, a rook, a bishop, or a knight." The chess lesson had ended and The Great Pawn Hunter and The Restless Knight went back to school.

A day went by and another letter arrived on The Great Pawn Hunter's desk. Inside the letter were shavings that looked like they came from the poor unfortunate pawn. It read:

"Cheese Please?"

The Great Pawn Hunter was so shook up that he decided to deliver the cheese. He placed some cheese by the base of the tree and climbed up into the branches to catch the Knapper! But all that came by was a mouse. He scurried up to the cheese, took a nibble, and scurried away. The next day The Great Pawn Hunter received another letter. It read:

"It's not Swiss cheese!"

Yes, the letter demanded Swiss cheese...the audacity. To make matters worse, a piece of felt, that looked as though it came from the bottom of the pawn, fell out from the envelope. The Great Pawn Hunter was in distress. He asked The Restless Knight what he should do. Restless said "Never give in to Pawn Knappers!" and the two came up with a plan.

They left the Swiss cheese at the base of the tree as demanded and went back to the school to await who would deliver the letter to The Great Pawn Hunter's school desk. However, after hours of waiting, who appeared on the scene but the mouse with cheese all over his whiskers dragging a letter. They couldn't believe their eyes. As the mouse scurried away from the school desk and into his mouse hole, the chess players came out from their hiding place. The Great Pawn Hunter opened the letter and out fell the pawn. A little bit shaken but none the worse for wear. The letter read:

**Mice are people too.
A birthday cake I'll chew.
As for who stole your little pawn,
you haven't got a clue.**

**So, listen to this mouse
I stayed up until the dawn.
I followed the Knapper to his lair
and came back with your little pawn.**

Well, The Great Pawn Hunter was delighted to have his pawn back and for the rest of his stay, until graduation, he left a piece of Swiss cheese with a birthday candle for the mouse to enjoy.

Heaven can't hold You
A poem

Heaven can't hold You.
Pages can't contain
The sum of Your works
whispers Your Holy Name
I reflect on Your Passion,
incensed by Your love.
The Spirit has a woman
as beautiful as a dove.
Her way bears a sorrow,
held up by Your Grace
that words can't express
and time can't erase.
In my heart, I know
He wants for her
every good thing.

And, dear friend,
that "every good thing"
is You.

The Great Pawn Hunter

The First Chess Tournament

Out from the mist, atop the famous hill, appeared The Great Pawn Hunter. Eager for glory, with the appetite of a man-eating lion, no ...ten lions, The Great Pawn Hunter descended on the town of Fehilach.

It is hard to believe it all started this morning. . .

6 a.m. screamed the clock. It is time to wake up. This was the morning of the big chess tournament. The Great Pawn Hunter put on a pair of jeans and pulled a wrinkled piece of paper from one of the back pockets. It read:

1. Push a pawn to the center
2. Bring your pieces off of the back row towards the center.
3. Don't touch a piece a second time.
4. Castle for safety
Coach

On the back of this message was scribbled:

Take pawns, lots of pawns, all you can eat and more! ...The Great Pawn Hunter

Just then, the phone rang. It was The Restless Knight. "Just calling to wake you up," said she. "This stuff about the center," replied The Great Pawn Hunter, "takes all the fun out of chess." "It's difficult to move when all the pieces are there." "I know," said The Restless Knight

The drive to the tournament was fun. The Restless Knight and The Great Pawn Hunter made faces at each other while trying to dodge invisible bullets shot from each others fingertips.

At the tournament, the players were paired.
"Pairings are up! for Round #1. Go to your tables and begin playing." said the Tournament Director. The Great Pawn Hunter went to the wall chart and found the first opponent: The Talker. As The Great Pawn Hunter sat at the board, butterflies danced and wild beasts roared in the hunter's stomach.
Okay, thought the hunter:
1) Push a pawn to the side of the board?
Now there was nothing that could quiet the great beasts.
2) Castle to the center.
The Ocean Swelled.
3) Touch the king a second time.
The clouds rolled in. Oh yeah, don't forget:
4) When in doubt take a pawn.

Everything felt right again!

With a bold thrust the first move was made .
1. h4

The Talker was quick in response to copy The Great Pawn Hunter's first move.

1) . . .   h5.

The Great Pawn Hunter - 41

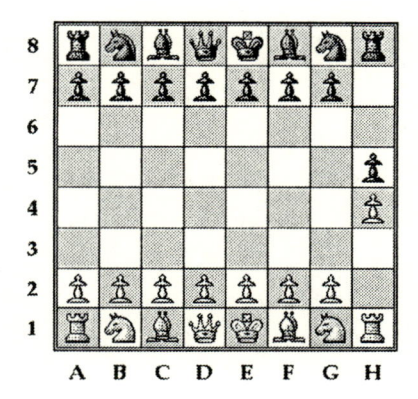

"Obviously, he must be a very good player, to play so quickly. I wish he would quit talking. I can't concentrate while he's doing that," thought the hunter. "Make your move!" said The Talker.
2. Rh3 was The Great Pawn Hunter's reply.
I wish I didn't do that. It's not what my coach told me to do. What did he tell me anyway?

2. . . .,   d6

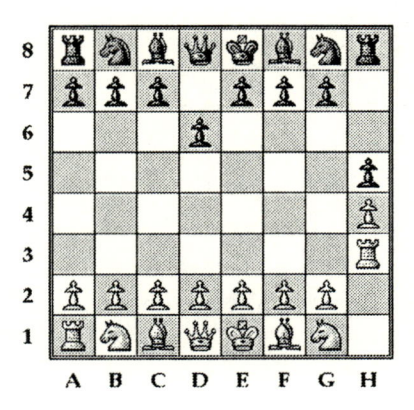

The Great Pawn Hunter - 42

Oh yeah, now I remember. Push a pawn to the center!

3. d4, Bxh3

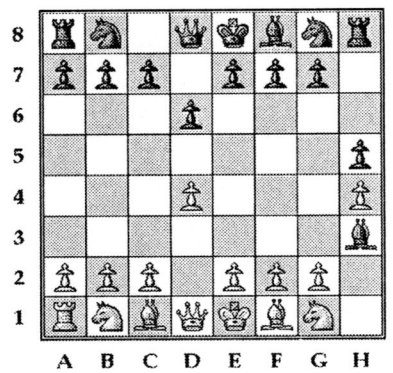

"OOPS! I didn't see that." said The Great Pawn Hunter. Clenching his fist, The Talker exclaimed "YESSSS!" and punched a hole in the air. The Great Pawn Hunter stared, in disbelief, as the captured rook was placed on the other side of the table. More losses and still more, a bishop, a knight, and then, gulp, the mighty Queen! To The Great Pawn Hunter, it felt as though the whole world was watching the game.

"OK, I have five minutes on my clock and The Talker has ... has... Hey, he didn't press the button on his clock yet!" The Talker's time was running out.

The Great Pawn Hunter quietly rose, walked over to his friend's table, and launched an invisible bullet from his fingertip at the time flag on his opponent's clock. ... It's good to be king.

Friends, when I was growing up, from time to time, my parents would have arguments over a disagreement. I thought they didn't love each other. But, one day I opened the door to the kitchen, after one of their fights, and found them embraced in each others arms and kissing affectionately. That's when I knew they were deeply in love with each other and it was their love that carried them through those tough times. So this next poem is in memory of them and it is for all those couples who are having a rough time of it. It is a testament of what it takes to survive. Sometimes, for the sake of love, someone has to give in. Although the poem starts with a knock down drag out fight, rest assured the king and queen are brought together and peace is restored in the kingdom once again.

God Bless us all.

A Clown with the Blues
(The Shrew Poem)

"I'm King of this board!"
said the King to the Queen
as she lowered the boom
on his head with a "Ting!"
"I'll have no more of that,"
said she to her clown
"Get off of this board
and here take your crown.
You're a slob and a louse
You are no more my spouse
than a dog to a cat
or a cat to a mouse!"
Now, the King to the Queen said,
"You're my love. You're my bride.
And, on my own board,
my head I'll not hide."
So, he turned his cheek
to the other side.
Well,
she hit him again
right smack on the nose
as a shiver went down
clear through to his toes.
And he fell on a square
as he said, "Please No Hun!"
and he was called out
at the count of one.
And the Queen exclaimed,
"No! what have I done?!"
and out from the castle
she started to run.
"Anything is better than

at the Kingside"
so she looked in the center
for a square there to hide.
And, that is why, friends,
she starts out every game
where her shoes
match her dress
and the square is the same.
And, the King, my dear friends,
is a "clown with the blues"
for he followed his queen there
for the sake of her shoes.
Yes, love is blind friends,
but it's better than hate,
and he loved his queen,
for she was his mate.
They were brought together
in the center of the row,
and they start every game
side by side, toe to toe.
So the next time you take out
that old grimy chess set
with a stain on the board
chewed and gnawed by a pet,
kiss the queen to the king
and then, take your seat
for in the center of the board
is where true chess friends meet.

The Great Pawn Hunter

Going to a Chess Club

The Great Pawn Hunter wakes. "Another morning without a plan," thought the Hunter. He called his friend The Restless Knight. "Hey, there's a great chess club downtown." said Restless. "Do you want to go? I hear there are grandmasters there!" The Knight, well, she always knew how to get the Hunter out of the house. "Cooool. I am there already." said the Hunter. "We could take the bus." said the Knight. The Hunter knew his pockets were empty. "I got a better idea, let's walk."

Much further along the way, just before you cross the tracks, was Old Maestro...They could see him now, plain as day...one hand out holding a cup and the other holding a sign. The sign read:

**One nickel, One thought.
from Old Maestro.**

The pawn hunter put down his chess set and rummaged around in his pockets. He couldn't find a coin. "Do you have a nickel?" said the pawn hunter. His anticipation was boiling over. When he got the nickel, he quickly dropped the coin in Old Maestro's cup. The man with eyes as grey as an old tin can picked up the chess set, handed it to the The Great Pawn Hunter, and whispered in The Great Pawn Hunter's ear, "It's all about space." Little did The Great Pawn Hunter know it would be the best nickel he never spent. Then it was The Restless Knight's turn. She dropped the nickel in the cup. Old maestro smiled at the Knight, took one long look at

The Great Pawn Hunter - 47

The Great Pawn Hunter and whispered in The Restless Knight's ear. He said "It's all about space." She giggled. They arrived at the chess club in a heated debate...ok an argument. "Is not," "Is too," "Is not," "Is too"...you get the idea. The day would have been ruined if it weren't for the woman who ran the club. She showed them pictures of past and present champions that were hung all around the club and introduced them to "Bughouse" a game for four players. "How do you play it?" asked the Knight.

Well, you use two chess sets side by side. You and your friend play on one side of the table against two players on the other side of the table.

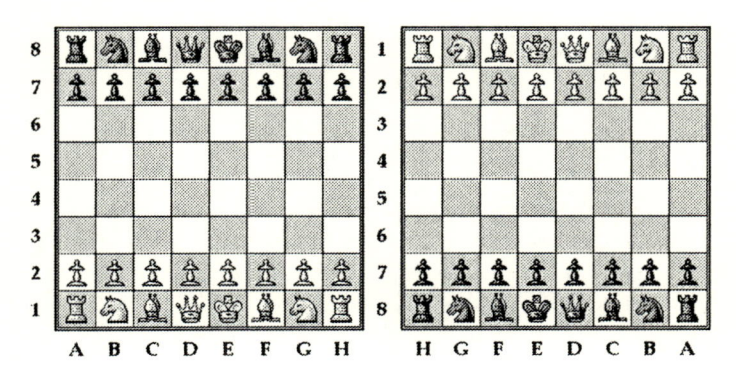

You have the white pieces and your team mate has the black pieces. Any pieces you capture from your opponent you give to your team mate and he can place them down on his chessboard. Any pieces your teammate captures will be given to you so you can place them down on your chess board. When it is your turn, you can either move or place a piece on your chessboard. Placing a piece on the chessboard counts as your move. You can not place the piece down on a square that is already occupied.

"What did she say?" said the Hunter.
"Just follow my lead." said the Knight.

The Restless Knight and The Great Pawn Hunter played many Bughouse games that day and made many friends. It was as they were leaving the club that they saw a photo of an old man holding a cup in one hand and a sign in the other. It was Old Maestro. And, the sign read "Champion" and the cup was a victor's cup.

Bringing Down the Choir
A poem

I'm bringing down the choir.
Not in tune Ya know.
The lyrics, they go up and down
where my vocal chords can't go.

I'd like to sing of majesty.
A humming bird on the wing.
But, my voice is predatory
killing birds and other things.

I'd like to sing "America"
from sea to shining sea.
But, I'm doomed to live a life of blues
screechy and off key.

Friend, if my prayer was heard in Heaven,
it would surely be
to sing the praises of my Good Lord Jesus
through all eternity.

For He rescued us from our sins
drawing His finger in the sand.
The Holy Spirit came among us
spreading truth throughout the land
God knows, when we get to heaven
maybe, lagging far behind,
I'll give a free cut to each of you
waiting there in line.

But friend, in line,
you will have to put up with
me and my "Rosary"

singing the praises of my Good Lord Jesus
screechy and off-key.

The Great Pawn Hunter

The Initiative

Winter is setting in. Snow flakes are falling. The Great Pawn Hunter is looking out through the glass and drawing something on the window with his finger. "What's that you are drawing?" said The Restless Knight. "You'll see...I'm not finished yet," said The Great Pawn Hunter. "I bet I can guess," said Restless. But, before he could finish, the librarian interrupted them. "Your chess coach is here...all of you go to the chess area." Well, the chess players almost jumped out of their shoes and ran towards the chess room.

The chess coach had something special to teach them today.
They were going to learn about "The Initiative!"

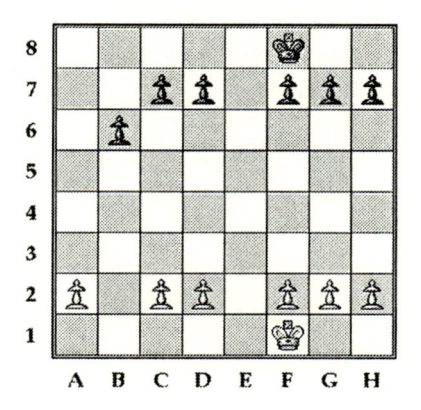

The above diagram shows white having three pawn islands...(a1), (c1,d1) and (f1,g1,h1). Since the a1 pawn has an enemy pawn on its neighboring b file, it can not advance up the file. Since it has no other

The Great Pawn Hunter - 52

helper pawns on files next to it, it can fall prey in the endgame to enemy pieces.

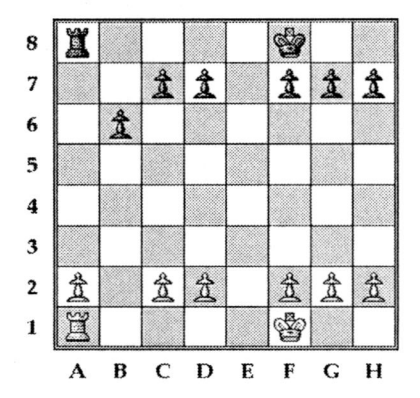

```
8 | ♜ . . . . ♔ . .
7 | . . ♟ ♟ . ♟ ♟ ♟
6 | . ♟ . . . . . .
5 | . . . . . . . .
4 | . . . . . . . .
3 | . . . . . . . .
2 | ♙ . ♙ ♙ . ♙ ♙ ♙
1 | ♖ . . . . ♔ . .
    A B C D E F G H
```

In the above diagram Black has a Black Rook attacking the weak a2 pawn. The player with the White pieces has to defend the pawn. Look at how little space the White rook has to move around in. It is stuck on the a1 square defending the pawn with nowhere to go. However, the Black Rook can move all the way down the (a) file to attack the a2 pawn or it can move sideways across the 8th rank. It could also move to the 5th, 4th, or third ranks and attack horizontally.

When you are on the attack you have something called, "The initiative." This is a fancy word for having the move that steers the game where you want it to go. Once you go on the defense, you lose that move. You lose the "initiative." When you force your opponent onto the defense, your opponent will have less space to run around in...and his pieces will get in the way of each other! The opponent will be more likely to make a mistake!

So, isolate your opponent's pawns. Attack the pawns and force your opponent on the defense...and keep the initiative!

Well, this struck a chord with The Great Pawn Hunter, but, the lesson was over all too soon and they had to leave. It was as they were leaving that The Great Pawn Hunter remembered his unfinished drawing on the window. He raced over only to discover...it had already been completed! He stared in disbelief...but there it was...just as he had imagined it.

♙

He shouted out to The Restless Knight "Did you finish my drawing Restless?" The Knight running towards the window said, "Yup, but who drew that?" "Who drew what?" said The Great Pawn Hunter. "Who drew the smile on the pawn?" said The Restless Knight. The Great Pawn Hunter stared at the drawing and through the glass he could see the snow settling on the ground and on an old man making his way up the street to turn the corner... it was Old Maestro...and the chess players whispered Old Maestro's words...

"It's all about space!"

The Grain in the Wood
A poem

One pawn white
One pawn black
stood at an angle
and clashed in attack.
Each pawn fought valiant.
Each pawn raised his sword.
Each wound up
at the side of the board.
And as each looked on
at the horrific fight,
one pawn black,
one pawn white,
one turned to the other
and let out a roar
"What on sixty four squares
were we fighting for?
We're both alike."
One sat.
One stood.
"The only thing different
is the color of the wood.
Our duties the same
our king is to reign
one God is supreme
bless His holy name."
And as the battle roared on
a king's flag would fall
while one pawn sat
and one stood tall
and one felt for the other
and consoled as he should.
It was for the love of his brother

he did what he could.

Players,
it's the grain in the piece
not the color of the wood.

The Great Pawn Hunter

The Mouse's Plan

"Catch!" shouted The Restless Knight, as the ball hurtled through the air. "I got it, I got it!" shouted The Great Pawn Hunter. Backward he ran, the sun shining in his eyes, the sweat coming down his brow, and like many a great ball player, ...lost the ball in the sun. It bounced on the ground and rolled through the bushes behind him.

On this day, a mouse was busy foraging for food by some bushes when ..."Kablam!" went the ball off of his unsuspecting noggin. He staggered left, he staggered right and then he fell...and there he was, out like a light.

"Oops!" said The Restless Knight. She didn't see the mouse, yet. All she was thinking was "Wow! I can really throw it that far!" It was then that she found the ball and discovered ...the tragedy!...and promptly started crying. "Did I do that?" sobbed Restless. The Great Pawn Hunter came running over to see what was the matter. "Wow!" shouted The Great Pawn Hunter..."You hit him square on the noggin." ...Well, she cried even louder and ran into the house. The Great Pawn Hunter had really put his foot in it this time. "What am I gonna do now," said he. "Mom, is really gonna kill me, deader than the mouse!" He walked over to the steps of the porch, slouched down on a step, and sunk his face into his hands.

Meanwhile, the mouse was starting to wake up. Just a twitch at first...then a deep breath...and then, target sighted, he made a mad dash through the door and into the house! Ya know, there are many ways to skin a chess player, and this mouse had something going for him, sympathy and a keen intellect. Every mouse knows this spells ...a full belly.

Down the hallway he scurried. He knew there was little time to execute his plan. Staying close to the wall, he darted into the kitchen. First going left and then going right, his feet slipping on the kitchen floor, he finally made it into the pantry..."Safe at last!" he thought. This was a piece of cake...hmmm, cake mix. There's a great idea...and after finding his cake mix and eating it too, it was time for him to go. So, he jumped down off of the pantry counter and was just about to leave...when...it hit him. No, it was not a broom, It was not a boot. It was the scent of...the call of...the allure of the sweet potato! "Ya know, there is always room for potatoes," he thought. First he had a nibble, then another, and then a big bite. He was in heaven! However, the mouse was not sticking to his plan of eating the cake mix and leaving. Slam went the front door...and a shudder went through him.

Down the hallway came The Restless Knight. The mouse's little heart was palpitating! He could hear her footsteps. She walked into the kitchen and ...opened the pantry door. Well, the mouse motioned to go left, and then he motioned to go right. His feet slipping on the pantry floor. That's when it hit him, or should I say he hit it...the sack of sweet potatoes. "Kablam!" and there he was, out like a light...again!

When he came to, he was lying in the garden. "What a knightmare," he thought. I must have imagined it. Little did he know, Restless had felt sorry for him.

She picked him up, ever so carefully, and carried him out to the garden where he remains eating sweet potatoes until this very day.

To Catch a Butterfly
A poem

Whiskey's eyes closed on the table
there beside my bed.
I wondered what was taking place
there within his head.
His limbs began to twitch and quiver.
He is fast asleep it seems,
trying to catch a butterfly
there within his dreams.

I whispered "I love you Whiskey.
Catch that butterfly for sure."
And, his tail began to zig and zag.
Soon, he began to purr.

"You little rascal Whiskey
on my table's end.
With an I.Q. greater than your owner's,
faking sleep is not that fair
my little furry friend.
OK, So you heard me tell you I love you.
Don't let it go to your head.
Giving me kibble won't forgive you."
I sternly, stubbornly said.
Friend, what can I do?
My cat's got an I.Q.
I could take him to court.
That's right. I could sue!
But, what if he won?
He'd have all the fun.
I'll settle for kibble
before it's begun.

Well,
Whiskey came over from the table,
cuddled up against my chest.
And, I made a tent for the two of us
where we both could rest.

Friend, a word of advice:
The Lion is King
and he's got a little Son
of which I do sing.
So, settle for kibble
out of court and be wise.
"Love is Love" from
dear Whiskey
or from
xoxo God xoxo
in disguise.

The Great Pawn Hunter

A Better Move

The stone skipped off the water. One, two, three hops and then a mighty KERPLUNK! and disappeared beneath the surface. The chess players had gone to the pond after their chess lesson was over. "Wow! Three hops, that was good," thought The Great Pawn Hunter. However, then he remembered what his chess coach had told him in the lesson earlier that day. The coach said, "Once you find a good move, find a better one!" Here is what the coach had showed them:

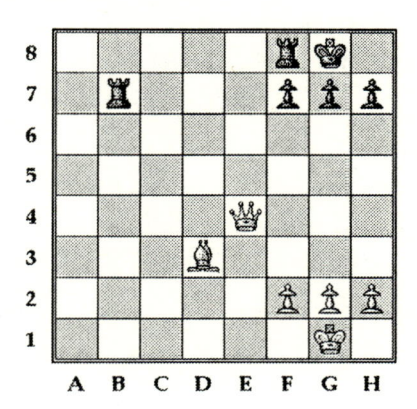

Taking the rook with the queen is a good move. However, there is a better move on the board and that is checkmating the Black King with **1. Qxh7** checkmate!

So staring down at all the pebbles on the shore, he started to sort them out...one by one. Hours and hours went by with no luck. He tried short ones, long ones, fat ones, and skinny ones but none could beat the "three hopper" he had found earlier in the day.

The Restless Knight came down to the shore to visit him. "Whatcha looking for?" said Restless. "I'm looking for a four hopper," said The Great Pawn Hunter. "How about this one?" said The Restless Knight. "I think it's pretty." and she opened her hand to reveal a beautiful white stone! However, The Great Pawn Hunter just kept on looking at the ground, searching in earnest. "Pretty, has got nothing to do with it!" said The Great Pawn Hunter. "You obviously have no experience skipping stones!" said he. Well, she got so mad that she threw the stone at the water and guess what... not one, not two, not three, but four hops off the water and an even mightier KERPLUNK! than the first one. She smiled an inward smile and walked away.

After she left, The Great Pawn Hunter searched and searched...and later that day, when Restless was eating dinner at her house, the doorbell rang. She opened the door and who was standing there but Old Maestro. The Great Pawn Hunter had asked him to give her a gift...and in Old Maestro's quiet and magic way, stretched out his arm, waved a twig over his fist, and opened his hand to reveal a beautiful white stone. It would be given to Restless to make amends and yes, friends once more. She smiled and invited him in for dinner.

To Rise and Play
A poem

The Black King
surveyed the battlefield.
Sixteen men would be lost.
He sounded for a bold attack.
Their lives it all would cost.

The White King
saw the chink in his armor:
The pawns around his foe
were far advanced.
That was the weakness
his opponent
didn't know.

The White King sounded
Flank attack!
And, all his men rushed in.
They gained for him
the victory.
They gained for him
the win!

Now, the White King
to praise his troops
upon the battlefield, he did ride.
Saw bleeding there, upon a square,
a dark pawn, frightened,
who would not hide.

The White King knelt down
,with compassion, and lifted
that lonely dark pawn's head.

The Great Pawn Hunter - 64

and he spoke to those around him
words of which he said:
"This Pawn's deadly armor
was made of grit and nails.
A yoke, a rope, a harness
from a kingdom dark, he hailed.
He heard once of a myth:
of a kingdom, light with love.
In the trenches where he fought
dark squares, paid for dearly,
with his very blood.
He'll lay forever now
with the one he chose to serve.
The poor wee lad it was a pity
He was made of grit and nerve."

And, as the King rose up
the pawn reached up
and touched his cloak,
only for a second.
And, the White King, moved with pity,
turned around and knelt beside,
the bleeding pawn who beckoned,
the pawn who wouldn't hide.

The pawn whispered quietly
to the King above,
"I heard once of a myth,
of a kingdom light with love.
Tell me now is this true?"
The King he nodded "Yes."
And a tear came down the King's cheek
Upon the pawn's head it came to rest.
And the King said,
"With this tear I baptize you
in the name of the Father

and of the Son and of
the Holy Spirit."
And, the wind whispered it
high and low
to all of those
who'd hear it.

The pawn's face, it grew brighter
and then he passed away.
He was laid down gently
in a chess box
to rise again some day.

Players,
these pieces bright
are in a chess box
at the side of the board,
neatly tucked away.
And, they beckon,
my friends,
to you now,

"Come rise with us and play."

The Great Pawn Hunter

The Bartender

A page from the paper seemed to have a life of its own, as it whirled down the center of town. First past the pizza parlor, then the train station, and finally coming to rest, in the gutter, by the door of the pub...

The bartender was on duty today serving up "Freedom in a Glass." He didn't notice as a small mysterious figure crossed the street and picked up the paper. On it was the chess section...

A barman saw the figure from a window. He came down from upstairs to see the action. "There's trouble," said the barman with a wink to the bartender. The bartender stared intently as the door creaked slowly open.

"Come to finish me off?" said the bartender. The Great Pawn Hunter smiled to the bartender and asked "Did ya make a move yet?" answering a question with a question. The bartender brought out a chess set from behind the bar. The pieces had already been set up and were engaged in ...mortal combat. "Give me a second to think," said the bartender. He looked down at the board and tried to make believe he had not studied the position.

Displayed are the moves and the board:
1. e4, e5
2. Bc4, d6
3. Nf3, Bg4
4. Nc3, g6?

The Great Pawn Hunter - 67

Well, the bartender had been thinking about the game for a week and his anticipation was bouncing off the glasses! "Now, let me see" and he quickly made his move...

5. Nxe5!

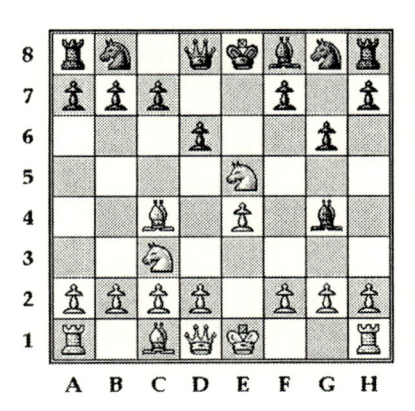

The Great Pawn Hunter was startled and then his eyes almost jumped out of their sockets. He flew his bishop down the diagonal and quickly captured the queen in half of a heartbeat...

5. ..., Bxd1

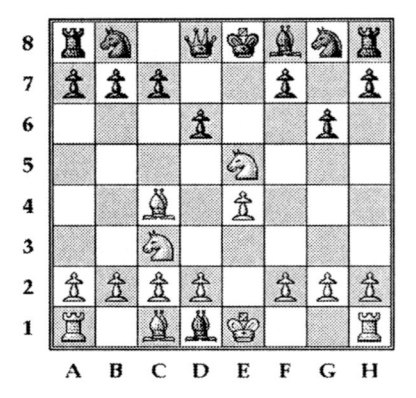

Well, The Great Pawn Hunter saw his mistake all too late, and he tried to put the queen and the bishop back on their squares...and when he did...he heard those words, the kind of words that make the hairs on a chess player's neck stand up... "Touch Move!" said the bartender with a friendly smile. "What do you mean?" asked The Great Pawn Hunter. "You see, when you touch a piece you have to move it. It's a law of chess." mentioned the bartender.

6. Bxf7, Ke7

The Great Pawn Hunter - 69

Well, the look on The Great Pawn Hunter's face could tell the whole story. But, I'll try to put it into words. You see, many of the greatest chess players of our time had fallen for this same sacrifice of the queen. Giants of the game, such as Capablanca, Chigorin, and Tarrasch were just a few who had been victims to moves such as these.

7. Nd5 checkmate

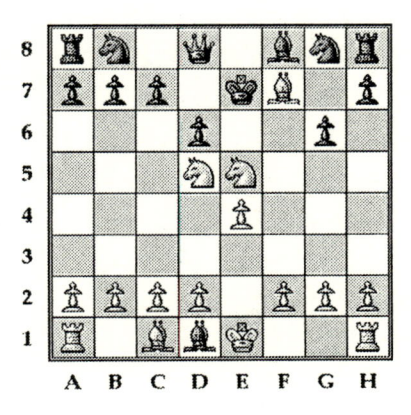

The Great Pawn Hunter shook hands, opened the door and stepped out onto the street. However, before he left, he scribbled a message on the paper he had picked up earlier and dropped it in the gutter. It read:

> **"So, here is my advice from me to you**
> **when you see a great offer,**
> **sit on your hands,**
> **and think it through!"**
>
> **The Great Pawn Hunter**

And after he had left, the wind picked up and whirled the paper down the street to a another small figure, with chess set in hand, as she made her way toward that very same doorway.

The Soap Box (e4) in the Middle
A poem

I once saw a pawn with good match sticks
rubbing them together for his king.
He said, "I'm trying to light a fire
on this chessboard,
a combination is waiting on the wing."

My king told me to stay here
on the Frontier line
while they pushed on up ahead
and to signal the attack with
these good match sticks
glowing embers fiery red

Now, it was nearly an hour
since he saw his king last.
Some say, bold attacks
are a thing of the past.
And, as enemy troops started to enter
a certain four squares on the board
called "the center."
Well, he thought he better
do something big fast.

So, he rubbed those sticks fiery red
and raised them high up above his head.
But, the wind picked up and
blew the flame dead!
Friend, the enemy was all around him.

He closed his eyes thinking he was lost
and sang out loud, "What is the cost?
Does the King have faith

The Great Pawn Hunter - 72

in good match sticks?"

Now, the battle roared on
and some would say
the attack was well played
for the King won the day.
But, you and I know
the true and only way.

(on his soap box indeed with a riddle.)

For the pawn stood his ground
and played his part
the matches blew dead
not the light of his heart
and he stopped the counter attack
through the middle.

Now, the King arrived back, after the attack,
and gathered his troops all around him.
For, the pawn's eyes were still shut
singing "What is the cost?" like a nut

(Tis no lie. Friend, that's
how they found him)

and the King stopped him short
brought him into his fort and said,
"...So, I have no faith
in good match sticks?!"
Well, if it were any other day,
that pawn would have paid I would say.
Indeed, for such a bold riddle.

But, the King smiled and said,

The Great Pawn Hunter - 73

(raising his hands above his head)

"I do have faith in good match sticks!
And, one match stick is You...
very bright and it's new.

(on his soap box indeed with a riddle)

For, you stood your ground.
And, we heard you all around.
on your soap box (e4) in the middle."

The Great Pawn Hunter

Free at Last

Crouching low by the side of the car, The Great Pawn Hunter whispered "Restless, do you see them yet?" The Restless Knight peered out from behind the bumper of the car. "The coast is clear," said she. They were looking for the other team in a game of "Relevio." Most all of The Great Pawn Hunter's team had already been caught and he and The Restless Knight knew there was only one chance of setting their teammates free... somehow, someway, someone would have to put their foot on the porch where their teammates were being held and shout RELEVIO! However, this was next to impossible without getting caught themselves...but, they had a plan!

The coach had shown them a tactic called the "Decoy" in a chess lesson a day before:

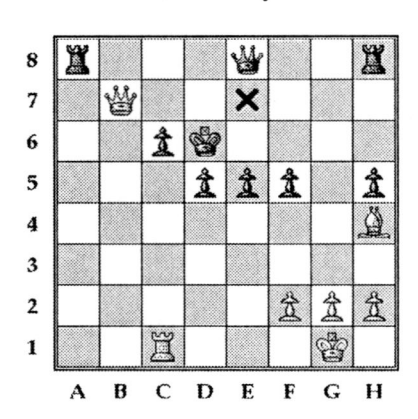

The (e7) square is protected by the Black Queen. If only there was a way to lure the Black Queen away from protecting this square. Then the White Queen could move to the (e7) square and checkmate the Black Monarch! The White Rook "decoy's" the Black Queen from protecting the King with

1. Rxc6!.

Black is forced in the reply 1)... Qxc6.

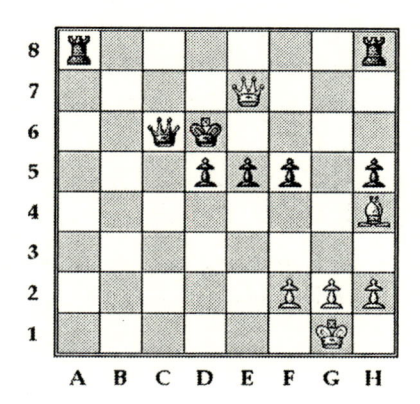

Now, the White Queen moves in for the kill with:

2. Qe7 checkmate.

So, slowly, they crept up along the sides of the cars until they could see their teammates being guarded by who else...none other than ...The Talker...and boy was he talking. "There is no way you can win now!" said he. "I bet the Pawn Hunter and The Restless Knight have gone home and forgotten all about you...what losers!"

But, the chess players had not forgotten their teammates and that is when they executed their plan. The Great Pawn Hunter came out from behind a car and into the street and shouted, "Hey Talker, does your Mother know you're a fool?" The Talker shouted back "She does not!" Well, the other players laughed and laughed, and when he realized what he said, he chased The Great Pawn Hunter down the street swearing vengeance. Well, they ran past the fire hydrant, and then the chess club, and finally past a small figure who waited till they went by to run over and place her foot on the unguarded porch and shout REEELLLEEEEVVIIOOOOO!!!...yes, it was The Restless Knight.

..and the captives shouted We're Free, We're Free, We're Free at Last!

What better way to end a day. 'Til tomorrow my friends, Joy and Peace to you all :)

The Sleepy Sire's Ending
A poem

The Fight!
Are you on the edge?
Black? or White?
"Stay in control."
It's on the King's mind.
It worries his very soul.

The edge without reason
is just cause for treason
when overload's the tactic
and checkmate's the goal.

How can one serve
when a king has no honor:
no pawns to shield him
while he sleeps in his sack.
And, his knights and his bishops
through decoy and ambush
lose square after square

"Keep pushing them back!"

from his sleeping lips,
the monarch he mumbles.
He is so unruffled
while others fight on.

One king in the center
That king he rumbles!
While the other king sleeps
behind rook and three pawns

And his pawn wall is dreaming:

The Great Pawn Hunter - 78

"No fight.
Easy pay.
Tomorrow's just another day.
He rules the roost," it would say.

When from the other wing they heard
cries of anguish from the sword.
And, the King woke up on the chessboard
to see his pawns had fled him.

And, his lordship's lips became a frown.

(Friend, you can't look up
when you look down.)

Checkmate is where it led him.

So, marshal your troops
Stay in control.
Fight for the center
Rumble!
And you will soon be winning the day
let the sleepy sire
mumble.

Shhh, don't wake him now.

The Great Pawn Hunter

The Clever Fox

Slowly The Great Pawn Hunter pulled back the window curtains. A small figure on the porch was about to ring the doorbell. Seeing an opportunity, The Great Pawn Hunter quickly shot down the hallway. However, as luck would have it...he tripped on the rug and flew headlong into the inner door...thud!, "Ahhhh!" came a voice from inside the house. The small figure's head lifted slightly..."Hmmm," thought the figure, "something's up!" Well, The Great Pawn Hunter picked himself off the floor and stumbled out to the outer door as quickly as he could.

"Ring!" went the doorbell. He waited. "Ring!" went the doorbell again. He waited some more. Then the figure put a hand on the doorknob and gave it a twist. The Great Pawn Hunter couldn't believe his luck. He quickly opened the door and shouted "Hi Restless!" with a clever smile on his face.

The Restless Knight walked right passed him and into the kitchen. "Pawn Hunter, are you there?" said she. "I am here," said he. "I guess nobody is home," said Restless. The Great Pawn Hunter shouted, "I am here!" Well, Restless paid him no attention and walked right past him on her way out. She closed the door and left him with a confused look on his face. "I am here!" said The Great Pawn Hunter. (with a whimper) ..."Unless, I am invisible...that must be it!" thought he...and the color came back to his face.

Well, the door opened with great speed once more and out bolted The Great Pawn Hunter onto the porch and down the steps. "I AM HERE!" shouted The Great Pawn Hunter...but, Restless was nowhere to be seen. He turned around, looked up onto the porch...and to his surprise, there before him was a note on the front door. "Checkmate!" it said, "meet me on the hill."

Now, up on the hill by the great tree stood Old Maestro, with people all around him. The Great Pawn Hunter arrived just as the old one was finished with his collection. He went over to The Restless Knight and together they listened to the old man's story. "It was a chase," he said, "the likes of which was never seen before and never since!"... "A mad dash toward the great cliff ran the fox, with chicken feathers still clinging to his chin. The hounds were close behind him. The horizon, far beyond the cliff, came rushing up to meet the fox as if to say "This is the end!". However, the fox did not alter from his path. Closer and closer he came to the edge and when the hounds closed in at ferocious speed, the fox suddenly turned right...and the men on horseback watched in horror as the hounds dashed over the cliff...every last one of them...and the clever fox disappeared, chicken feathers and all."

To Court in the Kingdom
A poem

The King lay on the table.
A pain within his chest.
He wasn't going to make it.
The Queen spoke to all the guests.

"My dear loyal subjects,
The King's had a bad turn.
He wandered too close to the action.
A lesson for all to learn.
Now, all of you my suitors
here to call on me
Well, I'm taking numbers
One and Two and Three.
You might call me progressive.
Please, don't think I'm excessive.
But, a Queen's gotta do
what a Queen's gotta do.
And, I know he's not dead.
But, He's pale in the head.
And, a Queen needs a King
to buy her a ring.
In short, for to court, in the kingdom."

Well, the clock ticked off the minutes.
Her suitors got into a fight.
The flag rose high on the clock face.
Rook and Pawn versus Bishop and Knight.
They clashed in the heat of battle,
suitors to the cause.
While, the King recovered in his castle.
A bit of gas was all it was.

The Great Pawn Hunter - 82

The Pawn showed up on her doorstep.
To the victor goes the spoils.
He gave the doorknob a twist
and kissed the King's wrist.
And, the King gave a shout
and ordered him out...

"TO THE FRONT!"

all to show for his toils.

Friend, take ear to the King.
Don't buy diamonds or rings.
And, if the queen tells you
"Come calling"
and gets you fighting
and brawling
Remember, my friend,
how the pawn met his end.

It's one move at a time.
One precious move at a time.
It's one move at a time
in the Kingdom.

The Great Pawn Hunter

Fried Liver

15)...Rh8 checkmate! "Fifteen moves! I won in Fifteen moves!" shouted The Talker! All The Great Pawn Hunter's friends heard the banter. How could you not? The Talker had announced it to everyone at the chess team finals. The Talker had played the "King's Gambit" Opening which The Great Pawn Hunter had never seen.

"Fifteen moves...I lost in fifteen moves," whispered The Great Pawn Hunter to himself. This was not The Great Pawn Hunter's day...and on a scale from 1 to 10 this was the equivalent of stepping on a rusty nail. The Great Pawn Hunter sat back and slumped into his chair, "Will this day ever end?" said The Great Pawn Hunter.

The Restless Knight heard his remark and came over to console her friend. "Could you help me study for my next match game?" said Restless. The Restless Knight had a simple and beautiful heart and was always thinking of others. "Study for your next match?...Who ya playing?" said The Great Pawn Hunter. "Guess who," said Restless, "The Talker." The Restless Knight knew how to get The Great Pawn Hunter out of his slump...and there was nothing better on God's Green Earth than winning the match against The Talker's team! "Okay, this is what you do. The Talker plays the Two Knights Defense. So, we are going to play something he won't expect...the FRIED LIVER ATTACK!" "Sounds gory, but if it will make him happy, I'll play it," thought Restless, and the coaching had begun. They spent over an hour on how to play the moves.

The Great Pawn Hunter - 84

Now the final round had begun and the moves starting the Two Knights Defense were as follows:
1. e4, e5
2. Nf3, Nc6
3. Bc4, Nf6

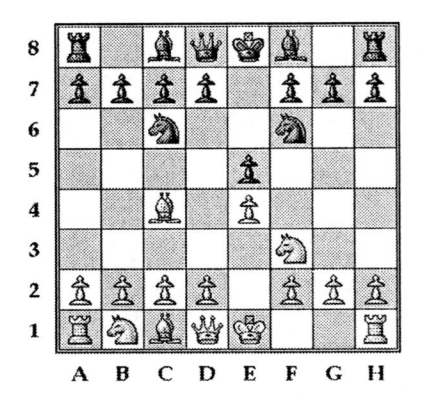

The Restless Knight played:

4. Ng5!

to enter into the Fried Liver Attack.
The Restless Knight's heart was pounding harder than a drum! She was awaiting The Talker's reply...

The Great Pawn Hunter - 85

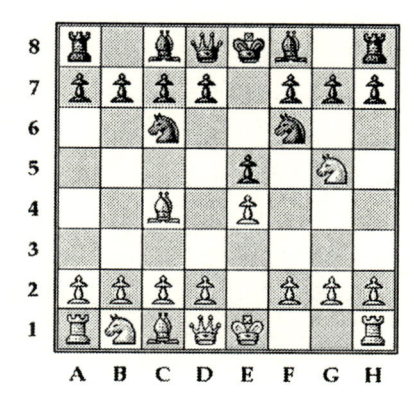

4. ..., d5
5. exd5, Nxd5

She couldn't believe it. Had The Talker read the book on the attack? "If he's read up on the attack, he'll surely crush me," thought Restless, and her heart beat even faster!

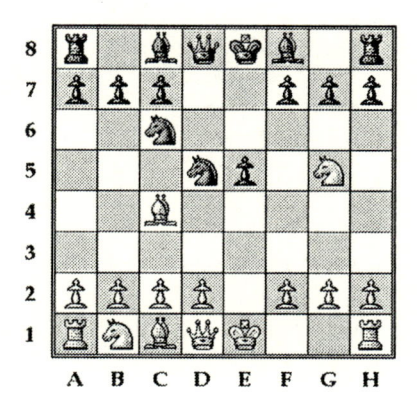

"Okay," thought Restless, "This is where the fun starts!"

6. Nxf7!

A stunning sacrifice!...attacking the Queen and the Rook at the same time! The Talker has to take the knight or lose a piece.

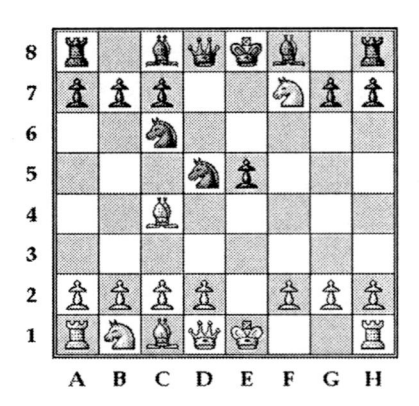

6. ..., Kxf7
7. Qf3+

"Check!" said Restless with humility only she could bring to the chessboard. The Talker's eyebrows began to twitch!

The Great Pawn Hunter - 87

7. ..., Ke6
8. Nc3, Ncb4

"Oh no, The Talker has definitely read up on the attack!" realized Restless.
"Go ahead, I'll beat a girl any day!" shouted The Talker.

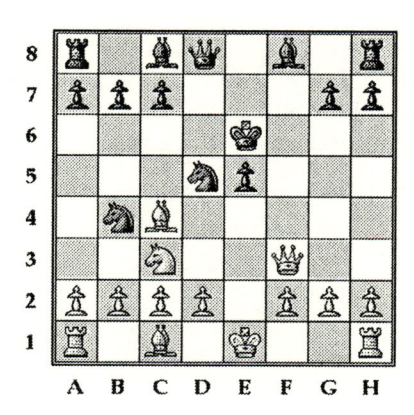

Well, this got The Restless Knight's ears burning.

9. a3, Nxc2+

10. Kd1, Nd4

"Put up or shut up!" shouted The Talker.

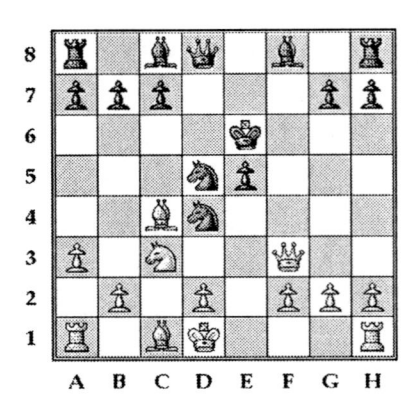

11. Bxd5+, Ke7?

She didn't realize it but her calm expression really unnerved The Talker. She looked over at The Talker and could sense his desperation! "Just deliver the goods," thought Restless, "or, should I let him off the hook?" She looked hard at the chessboard and ...and ...found 12) Qf7+ the crushing blow!

The Great Pawn Hunter - 89

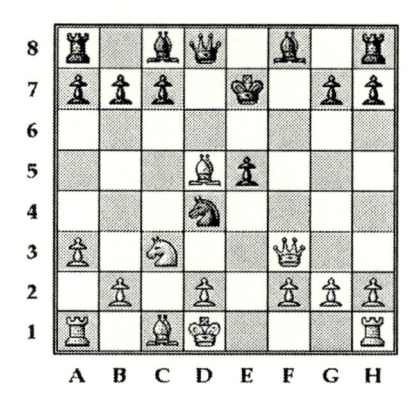

12. Qf7+, Kd6
13. Ne4++ Checkmate!

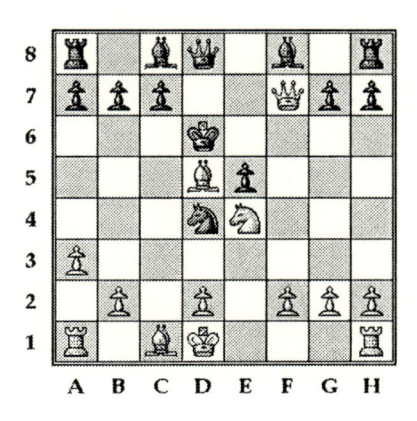

She offered her handshake to The Talker who shook it despite his bit of grumbling.

"Thirteen moves! I lost in thirteen moves!"

And yes, that day The Restless Knight had won the tournament for her team. When asked to comment, she said "It pays to prepare." and she smiled a humble smile, one that you see on people's faces when they are successful in life. How wonderful it is.

Once Upon a Center Square
A poem

Once upon a center square
in a game long gone away
a pawn scurried along a file
fearing death where victims lay.

Beads of sweat came down his brow.
He prayed to God above "Somehow,
save me from my plight.
I don't know darkness from the light.
Dear God, I've wandered off the file!"
He prayed this way for quite awhile.

And, as he prayed to curb God's wrath,
he met a stranger in his path
who didn't want to fight
for he knew the darkness from the light.

And, the pawn confessed to him there,
once upon a center square,
that he captured off the file
thinking that way was right
not knowing darkness from the light.

The stranger consoled him
out of book.
For, the stranger was
the piece he took.

The stranger said to him "Godspeed,
there are others you could lead
in the path of knowing right
discerning darkness from the light."

The Great Pawn Hunter - 92

And, the stranger piece
took a look.
Gave a safer variation
out of book.

And with joy,
the Pawn mentioned to him there
reflecting once upon a center square

"To know darkness from the light,
in the center, is the fight!"

'Twas the words out of book
spoken by him there
in a game long gone away
handed down to us this day
once upon a center square.
1) e4, d5!

"Make a good move now, my friend." says I,
"Capture and be captured!"

2) d4! in reply.

The Great Pawn Hunter

Brotherly Love

His cane stood in the corner now without the old man. The Great Pawn Hunter's Granddad had no use for it. You see he had gone for an operation the week before and received a new hip. Now, he was a cool guy!...the first on his block to have one. He was a charmer down at the hospital. All the nurses loved to stop bye and hear that Irish lilt of an accent. He even made swears sound divine and there were enough of those during the therapy. The pills were another story. Some pills were taken to ward off infection, but others, well, they had the unexpected gift of increasing the effect of his favorite Guinness Stout which, personally I think, added to that beautiful accent.

He was learning chess at the pub, yes, for the first time. His first task was to understand the chessboard and the moves of the pieces. This wasn't all that tough. You see, he had been an Irish checker champion. Once he had won so many games in a pub the stout keg had been moved to his table! ...They were playing for beer. As the beer was drank his game got better and better and his opponent's tempers got shorter and shorter. They got so mad that he had to lose game after game to escape with his life! Okay, a bit dramatic but, you get the idea.

The Great Pawn Hunter - 94

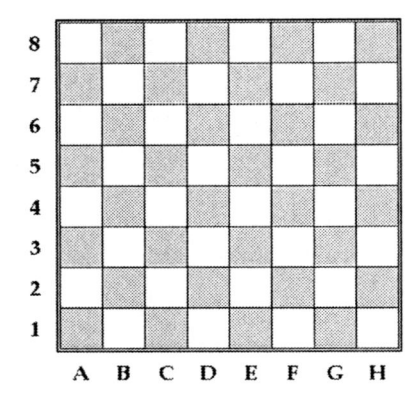

The bartender tried the direct approach. "The board," he said, "consists of 64 squares. Each square has a letter and a number that uniquely identifies it. For instance, the (b4) square." Granddad had interjected, "(b4)? What is (b4)? I know what comes after but not (b4)." said Granddad. The bartender could see he had a lot on his hands...and maybe he should shut Granddad off as well. However, Granddad had that ability, maybe he was blessed with it, to charm the beer out of any bartender. ...and this bartender was no exception. "Bartender," he says, "the time has at last arrived to inform you that I've been drinking in your premises for the past 20 years and you've always shown kindness towards me and I have never been shut off. However, I'll forgive you this once if you will only bless me with one more beer!" The bartender shouted, "Put your money away! Your money is no good here!" with a smile and a wink of his eye...and the bartender, for the sake of mercy, poured him another drink for free.

Yes, indeed, the Bartender was not the only master in the house that night.

The Stealth like Foe
A poem

A dark and dreary sight indeed.
Not a job for a noble steed,
waiting below the tower.

A finger grip
on an outcast brick.
A crack or crevice
to rest a hip.

Higher, steadily higher.

The Watchman lay sleeping
as the foe came creeping.
And, through the window, he did go
while his steed stood waiting down below
waiting for the stealth like foe
Who's passion burned like fire.

He gently came across the floor
and lay a rose abreast her door.
and the queen rose up from her bed
went to the door and softly said
"Come hither my King once more."
The knob did twist.
In the night, they kissed
and the King softly spoke to his lover:

"My Queen, I'm sorry for being late.
You see, I forgot my keys
and they locked the gate
and I climbed the castle to your room.
If you were there, I'd climb to the moon.

The Great Pawn Hunter - 97

But I must be leaving, it's daybreak soon
and the troops, they need my service."

He gently gave her a peck on the cheek
He said he'd be gone for a day or a week
and through the window he did sneak
waving goodbye to his lover.

Down he went, brick by brick.
A crack or a crevice to rest a hip.

Lower, steadily lower.

And, the Watchman lay sleeping
as the foe went down creeping.
And, his steed stood waiting just below
waiting for the stealth like foe,
who's passion burned like fire.
And, as he jumped down upon his steed
The gate did open
and he rode in to lead
the troops who need
his service.

And, the Watchman woke up
and he did stand
and found a pawn
resting in his hand.
He scratched his head
saying "Who? and When?
Goodness Gracious!
He did it to me again"

Now, the king didn't shout at him
and he never placed blame.
just a wink or two

for the love of the game.

And, He's winking at you
wishing "all of the same."

The Great Pawn Hunter

A Knight's Moves

There she was, off in the distance. She was small at first and grew larger and larger till she grazed right up to him. Sometimes, you are in the wrong place at the wrong time...but not this time. Moments like this are rare at best and The Great Pawn Hunter was savoring every moment. He sat there motionless and held his hand out to shoot the horse! "What are you doing?" said The Restless Knight. "I'm going to shoot the horse," said The Great Pawn Hunter...and he held out his hand, took aim, and snapped the photo. Well, the flash from the camera sent the horse fleeing from the roadside and into the wilderness. "Brilliant!" said The Restless Knight. "Maybe, I should shoot you too," said The Great Pawn Hunter.

His father once had medication. It was called a "horse shot." He told his nephew who called his father and said "Uncle shot a horse!" "You shot a horse," said his father. "Someone call a veterinarian!" What a commotion that was. As you can see, the grapevine around our parts leaves a lot to be desired.

Well, the chess team came back from their sightseeing and pitched their tents and the two chess players went over to the picnic table and set up their chessboard. The chess board had seen better days. It had been to many a campsite and once was almost used as kindling...Sacrilege! Much of the color of the chessboard had been worn off by pieces clashing in the heat of battle. In fact, they were engaged in a blitz game even as we speak. The Restless Knight

The Great Pawn Hunter - 100

was playing the White pieces and The Great Pawn Hunter was playing the Black pieces:

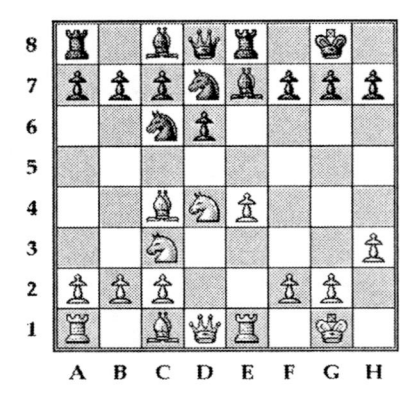

[Chess diagram]

Everyone knows that time in a blitz game is of paramount importance. The player with the Black pieces chooses what side of the board to place the chess clock on. Hitting the clock with the weak hand takes a lot of practice and usually takes more time off of your clock, that is, if it doesn't tip the clock over.

Since the king has no pieces in his area of the board, The Restless Knight made a stunning sacrifice.

1. Bxf7!

The Great Pawn Hunter - 101

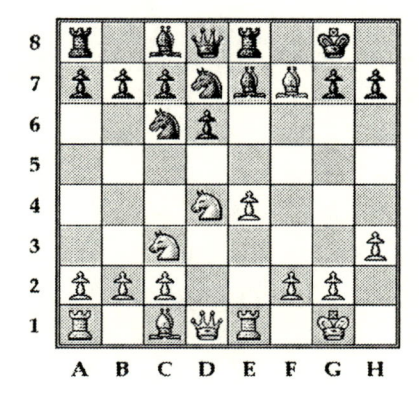

With this move Restless lures the black king out into the open. If The Great Pawn Hunter doesn't take the bishop, Restless will move her knight to (e6) and win the queen!

1. ..., Kxf7
2. Ne6

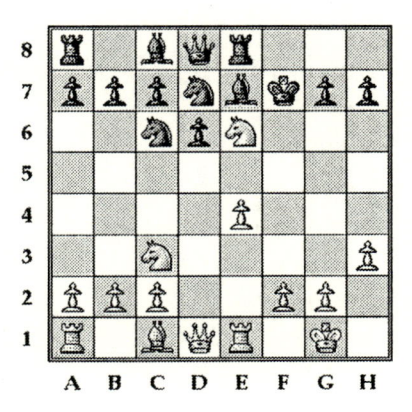

Ne6 attacks the queen which is smothered by her own pieces. "I'm gonna shoot that horse", said The Great Pawn Hunter. He reached out, snapped the knight off the board, and hit the side of the clock with his weak hand...It gave the clock a jiggle.

2. ..., Kxe6
3. Qd5 +

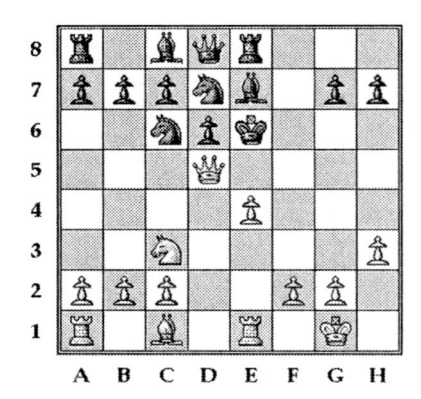

"Brilliant!" said The Restless Knight. "Now, I'm gonna checkmate you!" she said. However, she didn't hit her clock. She was too excited by the combination she had created. tick...tick...The Great Pawn Hunter just sat there and watched the time tick off the clock. A shrewd move by a devious opponent!

3. ..., Kf6
4. Qf5 ++

The Great Pawn Hunter - 103

With less than 5 seconds on the clock, The Restless Knight calmly reached over with her hand, and pressed her side of the clock and announced "Checkmate!" with an award-winning smile for an award-winning combination.

And The Great Pawn Hunter...well...he reached for his camera!

Wings of a Dove
A poem

Over the shapes
of chessmen she flew
from darkened squares,
forest green, a King knew
the battle was lost
and he raised a sigh.
He let go a dove and said
"Fly birdie fly

Tell the Queen
her love is no more.
Fly birdie fly
till you reach her door.

And let the Queen know
when the lillies bloom
and a gentle rain
on green squares
forms a dew,

I'll see her again
my lilly my love
fly birdie fly
so high up above."

The Song of war,
a hellish rattle,
drew our brave young lads
to the field of battle
and all that's left
is this message of love
sent to you my dear

on the wings of a dove.

> Fly birdie fly
> so high
> up above.

The Great Pawn Hunter

Standing Ground

Morphy T. Bear (the 'T' stands for "the") was quite a member of the family. He traveled from tournament to tournament and could always be seen looking at the chess game, from the side of the table, in earnest support for The Great Pawn Hunter. It didn't matter that Morphy couldn't play chess. It didn't matter that Morphy was stuffed either. All that mattered was that Morphy was there to console The Great Pawn Hunter in defeat or cheer as he marched onward unto victory!!!

History may state it differently, but I think it was that calm, determined look that Morphy radiated or maybe it was that cute, cuddly, all warm and furry attitude of his that so unnerved The Great Pawn Hunter's opponents. Your guess is as good as mine! I'll say this for him...when the chips were down, Morphy T. Bear brought to the table a unique qualification to appease even the most formidable of The Great Pawn Hunter's opponents or ...worse yet...tournament directors!

This occasion was no different as we join a game with The Great Pawn Hunter recently in session. The Great Pawn Hunter was playing the White pieces:

The Great Pawn Hunter - 107

In this game of speed chess, The Great Pawn Hunter's opponent, The Talker, was ruthlessly attacking The Great Pawn Hunter...what happened? Did The Great Pawn Hunter survive? ...Do birds fly? Do fish swim? If you swallow a frog can you jump higher? Lets see what happened in the game:

1. ..., Rxg2+ check!

a bold attacking move removing the last shreds of pawn cover from The Great Pawn Hunter's king... The Talker slammed the chess clock, with attitude, that shook the table. Morphy T. Bear slid slowly towards the enemy.

The Great Pawn Hunter - 108

2. Kxg2, Qh3+ check again!

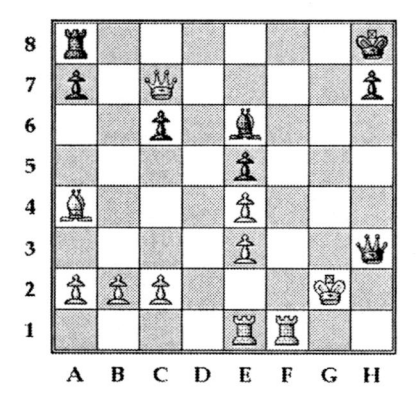

Ouch, that gotta hurt! Another piece, the queen, joined in on the action. "You're no match for me!" shouted The Talker. With no pawn cover, The Great Pawn Hunter's king was lunch meat. "Bam!" shouted The Talker as he hit the clock again...Morphy T. Bear slid closer!

"You're playing the wrong game," shouted The Talker. "You should be playing Marbles with that

The Great Pawn Hunter - 109

bear!" said he. Little did The Talker know that The Great Pawn Hunter was quite a good Marbles player and could beat The Talker any given day of the week!

3. Kf2, Qh2+ check again!

another slam of the clock...Morphy T. Bear slid closer still!

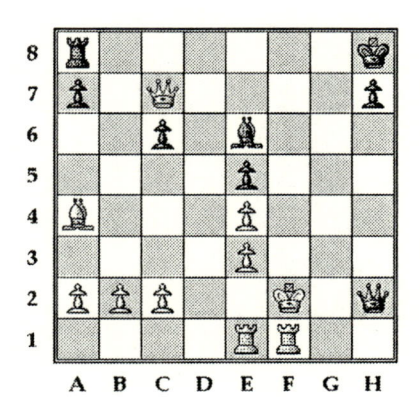

4. Kf3, Rf8+ check again!

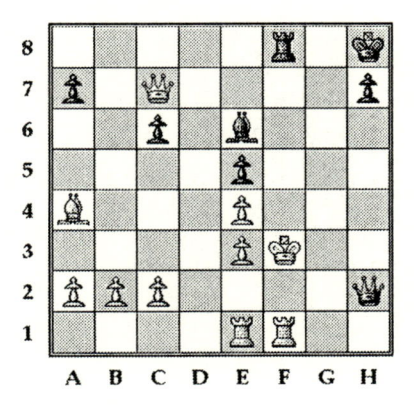

The Great Pawn Hunter - 110

With this final slam of the clock, Morphy T. Bear, with courage and determination far beyond his years, was finally within range right next to the Black Monarch.
5. Qf7 !!!!!!

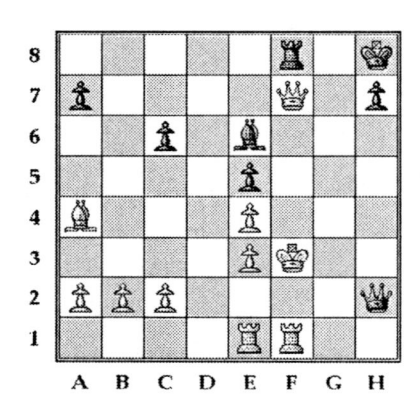

"Get that stupid bear off of the table!" shouted The Talker. He couldn't stand the look on the bear's face any longer. Quickly he reached for Morphy, who was standing ground, and The Talker hit his own king with his hand.

Over the king went crashing down on its side and, just as the king hit the chess table, O-P-P-O-R-T-U-N-I-T-Y KNOCKED. The Great Pawn Hunter shouted "I accept your resignation," and it was a good thing he did because 5)..., Rxf7 was checkmate! Yes, another game in the win column. So friend, when your game is on fire, and your pieces are hot, shout if you dare. But, don't mess with the mascot!

Players, near Boston Massachusetts, just over the river at Harvard Square in Cambridge, there is a coffee house named "Au Bon Pain" which in French means "The Place of Good Bread." Many chess players frequent there and you can always pick up a game outside at the chess tables. Most play "5 minute" blitz but I like a slower time control. 10-15 minutes suites me fine. I hope that you enjoy this little poem that I wrote for all of you who have ever played the game and the weather.

The Place of Good Bread
A poem

Two chess players met
to play the game.
One was from Medford.
One from The Plain.
They shook hands,
told each other their names.
They started the clock.
It started to rain.
One looked at the clouds.
One looked at the game.
Pitter Patter on the board.
"We'll get soaked to the skin.
Should we stay out? Or?
Should we go in?"

The man from The Plain
kept his head down
and stared at the cross
on his king's crown.
"I've got nowhere to move.
Lord, the game's in your hands."

The Great Pawn Hunter - 112

whispered the man from The Plain
to Medford Man.

Rook sac on the eighth
Makes way for the Queen.
Medford Man's eyes widened.
His glasses filled with steam.
And, they fogged up
while the raindrops kept pouring.
My friends, he couldn't see
the game before him.

Medford Man sac'd his Queen
instead of his Rook.
While the man from The Plain
gave Heaven a look.
"Praised be Jesus !" he stated
as he winked and he smiled.
Picking up Medford Man's Queen,
Praising God all the while.

And, Medford Man said
"You can do that?"
eyes widened and sore
"You can do that?"
as it rained and it poured
"Goodness Grape Juice, my friend,
You can do that!"

Now,
he
most surely found
Jesus.
for,
he
believed

in the score.

The Great Pawn Hunter

Bugology, The Great Escape

"Oh, it's a bug!" shouted The Restless Knight. The Great Pawn Hunter and she got together to do their homework. Now, homework and chess was on The Great Pawn Hunter's mind but he quickly realized that if he didn't take care of this bug neither task would be completed...and the quest began!. Quickly, he sprang into action. He ran over to the bug, lifted his foot, and stepped onto its..."Don't step on it!" shouted The Restless Knight. "Well, what do you want me to do...give it a name?" said The Great Pawn Hunter. Well, as is now widely known, The Great Pawn Hunter lost the quarrel and "Poor Fred," as the bug shall be called from here on in was to be brought outside per order of The Restless Knight. The Great Pawn Hunter's eyes rolled up into his head, much like the bug. He had visions of what Poor Fred might look like under a magnifying glass...with the sun beaming down at just the right angle. But, that would have to be put on the back burner. The Restless Knight had pardoned Poor Fred, for being his buggy self, and there was nothing The Great Pawn Hunter could do about it.

Well, The Great Pawn Hunter stepped onto a stool to find a cup. "But, what about Poor Fred?" asked The Restless Knight. The Great Pawn Hunter answered back, "Be calm, I know what I am doing. I have a plan!" as he scrambled to grab a cup from the cupboard. "Here is a piece of paper," said Restless. "You'll need it," she said. Neither player knew it was The Great Pawn Hunter's homework paper entitled, "My life and Games," but, I digress. Now, Restless wanted to bring Poor Fred outside because it was her nature and The Great Pawn Hunter wanted to bring Poor Fred outside too...and then step on him. Subtle differences...go figure.

Soon, the plan started to unfold. The Great Pawn Hunter ran over to Poor Fred and began lowering the upside down cup over the bug's head. Well, Poor Fred shot out from underneath the cup and made a mad dash for freedom at one hundred bug miles/kilometer's per hour...that's about (1 inch/2.5 cm's) to you and me. "He's getting away!" shouted The Restless Knight. "Don't worry!" shouted The Great Pawn Hunter and he placed the cup down around Poor Fred. Now, you could hear Poor Fred racing around in circles inside the cup. Then, all at once, he stopped...and there wasn't a sound to be heard from Poor Fred. Minutes went by. "Maybe, he is dead," said Restless. "Give a look see," said she. The Great Pawn Hunter's eyes rolled up into his head once more and...he lifted the cup!

Sensing the opportunity, Poor Fred sprang to life and made a second more mightier dash for Freedom. Quickly he darted towards the wall at 200 bug miles/kilometers per hour...that's about (2 inches/5 cm's) to you and me. It quickly became evident that Poor Fred wasn't going to get away. The Cup's shadow overcame the bug and there he was trapped again. I tell you folks, "What's a bug to do in a great country like this?"

Now, the second phase of the plan was put into action. The piece of paper was placed onto the floor next to the cup and within a moments time The Great Pawn Hunter slid it underneath the cup and Poor Fred too. Loudly the players rejoiced. But then, the chess players realized something. Someone would have to carry the cup and paper outside where freedom awaited for Poor Fred. "Here, you do it. I don't want to do it. You do it," bickered the chess players. "Well, you got the cup," said The Restless Knight. "Well, you got the paper," replied The Great Pawn Hunter. Negotiations seemed stretched at best. "Okay, let's draw straws, they decided. As you would expect, The Great Pawn Hunter wound up with the short straw. He picked up the cup and paper and carried Poor Fred outside to cheers from the neighbors who were glad to see peace restored and a good deed done.

However, when The Great Pawn Hunter lifted the cup from the paper, Poor Fred was nowhere to be found. Only a chip on the rim of the cup was left. Some people say that a villain had done Poor Fred in. Some people say The Great Pawn Hunter had ulterior motives. But, I think Poor Fred, mastermind that he was, summoned all the strength in his little bug body, and chipped his way out to freedom! That's this man's opinion.

P.S. As for The Great Pawn Hunter's homework...Poor Fred rated it a "B", uggy.

Inside - Out
A poem

Quarrels have an awkward bent.
You don't know where your temper went.
You shout and scream.
You raise a fist.
You can hurt your heart.
You can hurt your wrist.
So relax a little.
Take a rest.
And more than that,
don't be a pest.
For quarrels are friendships
turned inside out.
For this I'm sure,
there is no doubt.
So, laugh a little, hug a little,
kiss a little, love a little...
and you'll radiate a smile
all about.

The Great Pawn Hunter

Zugzwang
A Halloween story

Ah! sweet cemetery...loveliest roses of the field. Never the shame of flowers, plucked from the graves, in the name of perpetual care, shall lay abreast your doorstep. For you see, beautiful flowers will never send prospective buyers away from an advertised grave plot. But, the withered ones will. However, a poor meek grave digger didn't think it was right to throw withered flowers in the dump when they still had good roots...and so begins our story...

One day he gathered some withered flowers thrown from graves and especially from one grave of an old chess player he once knew and brought them home to his family. They became a beautiful rose garden.

Now, one night he had a dream. The grave digger was being chased by a gang he couldn't escape from. He moved from avenue to avenue falling over the cobblestones in a desperate plea to escape from the mysterious figures. They were closing in on him. He fell to the road scratching the ground in a feverous attempt to right himself with the backs of his hands and feet. The gang closed in above him. His heart was beating wildly. Never in his life did he feel such dread. There was no way out. It was the endgame. All the moves he had left, were bad ones. He was in "Zugzwang". He prayed to God. He shouted "God where are you?" and just as his doom was imminent he awoke!

He kicked the clothes off of his chest and looked around him. He was covered in sweat. The room was dark but with the light that shone from the clock, he could see an outline.

Now, as is widely known, ghosts can be seen from twelve midnight to two o'clock in the morning. But, after two o'clock, they must go back to their resting place, not to appear outside of their grave till the following night. But it was only 1:57 am! He had three minutes left.

Slowly, this outline came out of the shadows and into the light. The grave digger studiously watched the figure's every move. As it came closer, he could see the dim light pass right through the figure's face. The face was that of an old man, wrinkled but strong of character. The spirit moved beside the bed and began to bend. The grave digger began to pray. But he did not pray for himself for the grave digger always thought of others. He prayed for God to give the spirit rest.

However, for this spirit there was no rest. He had come for two goals and he had already obtained one of them. For you see, the spirit was the old chess player he once knew. It was the spirit that gave him his nightmare and it was the spirit that saved him from it, and it was the spirit that caused him to pray...a guardian angel, a teacher, a friend.

As the grave digger prayed, the spirit peered over the table beside the grave digger's bed. On the table was a lamp. Beside the lamp was a pawn. Beside the pawn was a chessboard. Beside the chessboard was a crucifix. Beside the crucifix the spirit found what he was looking for. For beside the crucifix was a beautiful red rose brought back to life...his rose!

The Great Pawn Hunter - 120

The spirit's eyes smiled. That rose was planted by his family in loving remembrance. The spirit wanted it back and was prepared to fight for it. He beckoned to the grave digger with his hand to rise and play a game of chess. The grave digger got up and sat at the board, half believing the events before him. He motioned with his hand to set the chess clock, but, the clock set itself...for three minutes...and the game began:

The Spirit's deadly "Night Attack!"

1.e4, Nf6 2.e5, Alekhine's Defense
Nd5 3.Nf3, d6 4.d4, Bf5 5.Bd3, Bg6 6.c4, Nb6

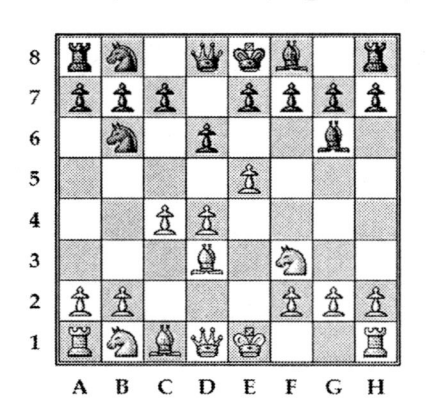

The Spirit playing white had a plan. He knew the loss of the grave digger's Queen's Bishop would invoke the launching of a deadly "Night attack!"
7.Bxg6 hxg6 8.e6

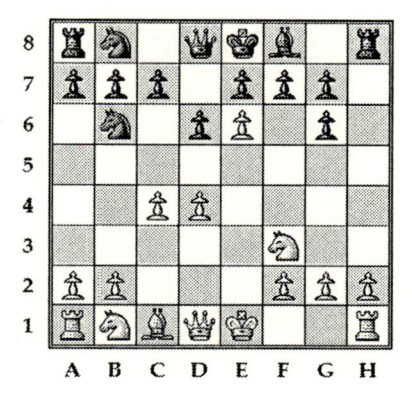

if fxe6? then the pawns on e6 and g6 will seal in the grave digger's pieces and his fate along with it.

8...f6 9.Qd3

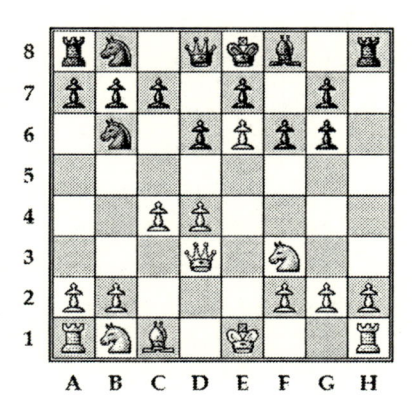

The spirit quickly developed with a threat against the weak pawn on g6!

9...Qc8 10.Qxg6+, Kd8 11.Qf7, Nxc4 12.Nbd2, Nxd2 13.Bxd2, g5 14.d5, c5

The Great Pawn Hunter - 122

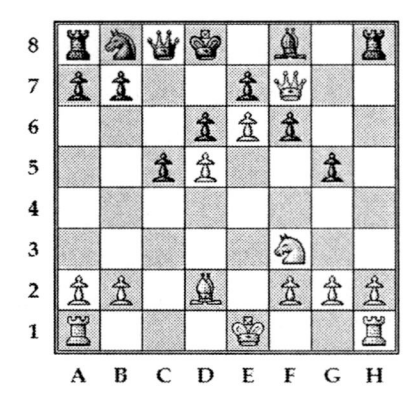

The grave digger desperately tried to give his king some breathing room.

15.Bc3 The threat?...Bxf6!
15..., g4 16.Nh4

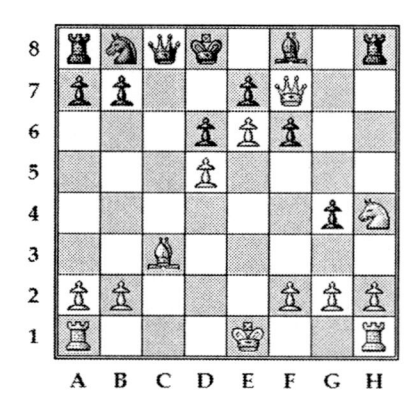

A wonderful move! The grave digger can not prevent the knight from moving onto the g6 square, removing the defender of the bishop. The grave digger must take the Spirit's knight.

The Great Pawn Hunter - 123

16...Rxh4 17.Qxf8+, Kc7 18.Qxe7+, Kb6 19.Qxd6+, Kb5

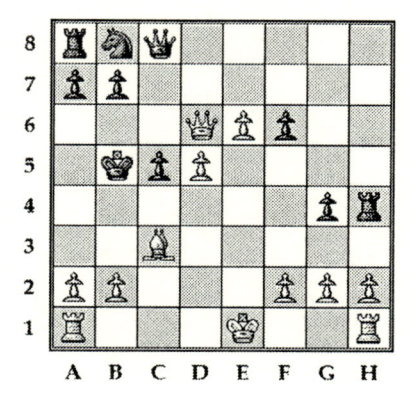

The grave digger's king was badly exposed...it was only a matter of time!

20.a4+, Kc4 21.Qf4+

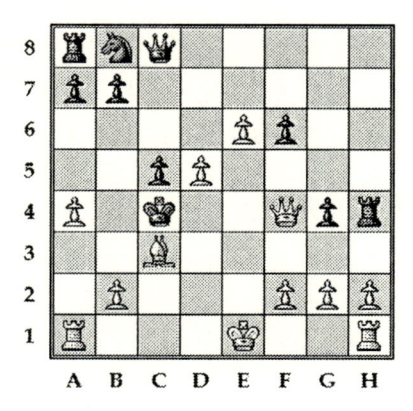

The grave digger's king was in jeopardy. There was no way out. He was in Zugzwang! So, he calmly

The Great Pawn Hunter - 124

and bravely met his fate. However, before his king passed from this world, he defiantly took a pawn!

21..., Kxd5 22.0-0-0+

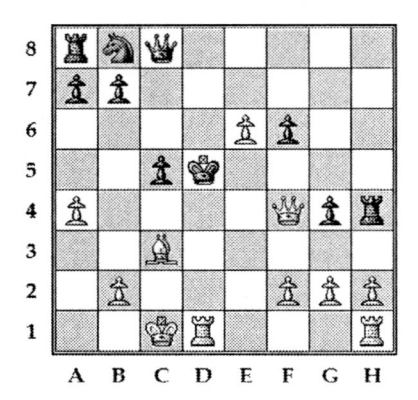

After Kc6. **Qd6** checkmate! After Kxe6. **Qxf6** mate
1-0

The two o'clock hour struck and the ghost disappeared. The next morning the grave digger took the rose and planted it at the grave of his chess playing guardian angel. After he planted it, he bowed his head. He offered a silent prayer and he was never more chased by fear of the unknown again.

Fighting the Good Fight
A poem

Some are called
and some are sent.
Here is where
the reason went:
"It's not if you win
or if you lose.
It's that you play
and your *intent*."
So, struggle through
and study too
and you will see
a newer you.
And when He comes
to judge with light,
you can say
I fought a good fight.
Stronger, faster,
You can be this master,
strong in heart
and mind of might.

The Great Pawn Hunter

Harmony
A Christmas story

It was Christmas Eve. The Christmas tree had been decorated now, soon to be the center of attention, in the Christmas frenzy of opening presents. The Great Pawn Hunter sat in his chair motionless beside the tree. He stared, in quiet expectation, before that special night...the night that Christ was born of a virgin...

She was scared at first, imagine...talking with an angel of God, but then, with humility, the virgin accepted God's plan for her life and her role in mankind's salvation. Old Maestro had told The Great Pawn Hunter and The Restless Knight "If you want to know Jesus, get to know, this virgin, his mother." "What is her name?" asked The Great Pawn Hunter. "Her name is Mary," said Old Maestro. Then he said to them "If you ever sin, seek her out. For with one word from Mary, Jesus will restrain his justice, for she is the Mother of Mercy and the Queen of Heaven. Through her, your prayers are heard quickly because God has chosen to honor her in this way." "The Queen of Heaven," said The Restless Knight. "Yes," said Old Maestro.

"Old Maestro," asked The Restless Knight "What is sin?" Well, he tried to explain. Old Maestro said, "It is the lack of harmony." "Old Maestro," asked The Great Pawn Hunter, "What is harmony?" Well, Old Maestro could see he was getting in too deeply and so he implemented the decoy maneuver. He handed them his presents.

The Great Pawn Hunter - 127

With expectations of the child inside each of them, The Great Pawn Hunter and The Restless Knight, gingerly unwrapped their presents. When they took the wrappings off the presents, each discovered a beautiful queen chess piece. They were overcome with excitement, for they had a gift from Old Maestro. They wanted to give him a gift as well. They knew Old Maestro had lost two pawns weeks before. When he opened his present he found just what he needed to complete his chess set. Yes, my friends, they each exchanged "Queen for a pawn" and with his chess set completed, Old Maestro decided to give them a chess lesson.

However, The Restless Knight still had the question on her mind and she asked him again "Old Maestro, what is harmony?" Old Maestro was being cornered in. He said to himself, "They want to learn about harmony? I will try and teach them with chess." "Harmony in chess," said Old Maestro "is when you connect the invisible paths of each of your pieces."

In the diagram, the white rook and bishop have some harmony because they overlap their paths on the

The Great Pawn Hunter - 128

(d8) square. The Great Pawn Hunter replied "But, there is a black knight that is blocking the rook's path on the (d) file." "Yes, that is true and that is the problem." said Old Maestro. "For your pieces to have true harmony, all you have to do is clear the invisible paths of your pieces and your pieces will be able to work together. In this example, the black knight on (d7) must be removed from the (d) file." said Old Maestro. "Do you have a solution?" asked he.

The Great Pawn Hunter and The Restless Knight put their heads together and came up with a solution. However, it would mean that they would have to give up their Queen. After the present that Old Maestro gave them, they didn't want to part with her. But Old Maestro instructed them "It is the sacrifice of the Queen that brings harmony to the pieces." Well, Old Maestro thought they had learned their lesson. They moved the queen to (b8) and the black knight was decoyed from the (d) file.

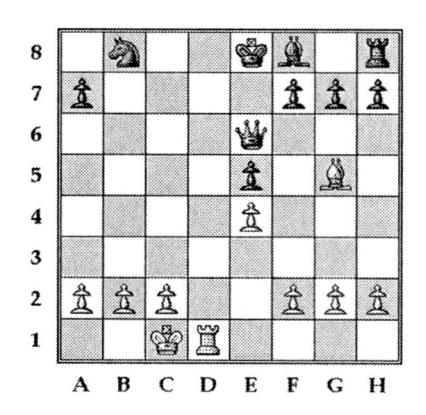

Now the white rook had its path cleared. "Do you see the answer now?" asked Old Maestro.

The Great Pawn Hunter - 129

"Yes," said the chess players. They moved their rook to (d8) for the checkmate, but Old Maestro was not out of the woods yet. "Does that mean we should lose the Queen of Heaven to our opponent?" asked The Restless Knight. Old Maestro was definitely cornered in now. His mind churned and churned and finally he answered her. "No," said he, "She is always with us. It is the sacrifice she makes with her prayers to Our Father in Heaven, because of her love for us, that helps unite us all and brings us true harmony." Well, the chess players were satisfied and the lesson was over.

A week went by. Around the Christmas tree, became quiet. It was lost in the light of a New Year. The delicate ornaments were still clinging to the tips of its branches like shy children to their mother. The ornaments didn't want to let Christmas go and neither did The Great Pawn Hunter! He gathered some thread and taped it to his new chess piece. He formed a hook out of a paper clip and attached it to the thread. He slowly rose, walked over to the Christmas tree and gently hung the queen onto one of its branches. The Great Pawn Hunter sat down, motionless, as he did on Christmas Eve. Staring in quiet reverence, beside the tree, he reflected on the lesson he had learned.

An Angel on Top
A poem

Christmas trees
can make you sneeze.
They're meant to be
outside in the breeze.
But, when you pick one
from the crop,
it simply looks great
with an angel
on top!

The Great Pawn Hunter

Battle on the Mountain

The mysterious sound of erratic clicking rang out from the mountain top. It echoed down the hillside and across the meadows through the valley and beside the streams. Slowly it returned to its owner, achieving the purpose for which it was meant, bringing with it chess players from every walk of life.

A small figure was busy in her garden doing chores when she heard the echo. The Restless Knight raised her ears and dropped what she was doing. The The Bad Bishop could wait another day...

The Great Pawn Hunter was in his room studying openings when he heard the echo. He quickly cleared his chess mat of pieces and rolled it up. He put the pieces into a bag and darted out of the room with anticipation and chess set in hand...

The Talker was in the school playground smoking a cigarette and causing panic, as per usual, when he heard the echo. He took one last pull from the cancer stick, dropped it on the ground, and crushed it with his foot. There was bigger game in the land. "Chess for Blood" is what they call it. He didn't play for sport or fun but to break a person's will. "Vengeance is mine," shouted The Talker to the mountain "and I shall have it!"...

The chess players met at the base of the mountain at their rendezvous point. The Restless Knight asked The Great Pawn Hunter "Do we have everything?" The Great Pawn Hunter replied questioningly "I think so" The Restless Knight grinned "Let's go through our checklist." Now, The Talker was watching them through his binoculars. "Do you have water?" asked The Restless Knight. The Great Pawn Hunter replied "Nope." She asked "Do you have a flashlight?" The Great Pawn Hunter replied "Nope." "Do you have an extra pair of socks?" The Great Pawn Hunter replied with a resounding "Nope!" "Well," asked The Restless Knight "What do you have?" The Great Pawn Hunter replied "Cheese doodles, Potato chips, Cupcakes and Twinkies!" The Restless Knight looked up at the sky and then at The Great Pawn Hunter and said "I can see you brought the essentials." The Great Pawn Hunter replied "Only the best."

The chess players walked up a smooth path leading to a tree with the trail markings on it. When they got there, The Great Pawn Hunter asked, "What trail do we pick?" The Restless Knight replied, "We must pick the trail with the green circle marker. It is the easy trail." Well, the green circle marker was pointing to the difficult trail. The blue square marker was pointing to the trail with medium difficulty. The black diamond marker, reserved for difficult paths, was pointing to the easy trail.

Through the binoculars, The Talker was smiling a mischievous smile and talking to himself. Whatever he was saying he was quite pleased by it.

Well, the chess players chose the trail with the green circle and disappeared into the trees to follow the trail. The Talker exclaimed, "Yes!" He raised his binoculars and walked around in a circle as if he had just pinned a mighty wrestler to the mat.

Meanwhile, the chess players were busy jumping from rock to rock, steadily moving upward. Hours later, they emerged from the tree line. When they saw the steepness of the grade before them, they had realized they took the wrong path. "Restless, someone doesn't want us to get to the top." stated The Great Pawn Hunter. They looked at each other and both said together..."The Talker."

Well, they were about to go back down the mountain when The Great Pawn Hunter spotted a small chalk outline of a pawn on a tree beside the path, pleading them to follow it. One pawn led to another pawn and that pawn led to another one. They counted sixteen pawn markers in all, a fitting number. But, finally, the pawn markers ran out! "What do we do now?" asked The Restless Knight. The Great Pawn Hunter said in a very convincing way "I don't know. Let's go back." However, before they turned back, they heard the echo of erratic clicking sounds beckoning them to continue and leading them onward!

Two hours later they were at the summit. They could see the figure of an old man entering a small stone castle at the top of the mountain. It was Old Maestro. "He certainly gets around doesn't he." said The Great Pawn Hunter to The Restless Knight. "Yes, he does." said she.

They followed Old Maestro into the castle. The erratic clicking sounds could be heard in a whispering roar coming from countless chess clocks being used in the heat of battle! The clocks belonged to mountaineering chess players from all over the countryside.

The Great Pawn Hunter - 135

The Great Pawn Hunter and The Restless Knight took a half point buy for the first round. It's not too often you get a chance to be on top of a mountain. They went outside and watched a beautiful eagle soar on the wind.

It was The Restless Knight that played a game against The Talker that day. The Talker had three points going into the following game and The Restless Knight had two and a half. The Talker played the white pieces and The Restless Knight played black.

1.d4 f5 2.Bg5 h6 3.Bh4 g5 4.e3 Nf6 5.Bg3 e6 6.Bd3 Nc6 7.Ne2 d6 8.Nbc3 e5 9.d5 Ne7 10.f3 Nfxd5 11.Nxd5 Nxd5 12.Bb5+ c6 13.Qxd5 Bd7 14.Qd3 cxb5 15.Nc3 a6 16.0-0-0 Be6 17.Nd5 Rc8 18.e4 f4 19.Be1

The Talker's white knight is too powerful and must be removed.

19...Bxd5 20.exd5 Qf6 21.Bc3 Kf7 22.h4 Bg7 23.b3 gxh4 24.Bb4

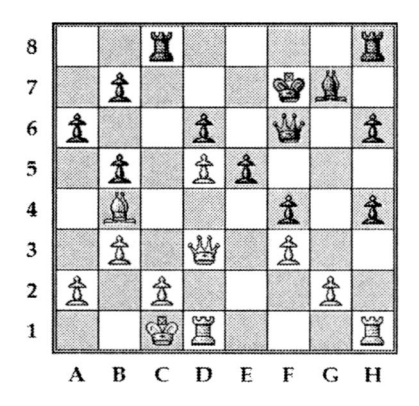

With 24...e4!, The Restless Knight playing black launches a deadly attack with the clearance sacrifice of the (e) pawn.

24...e4 25.fxe4

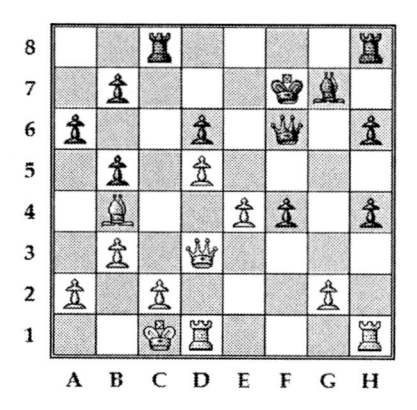

The Great Pawn Hunter - 137

If the pawn structure surrounding The Talker's king could be removed, The Restless Knight's pieces on the a1-h8 diagonal would be overwhelming.

25...Rxc2+ 26.Qxc2 [26.Kxc2 Qb2#]

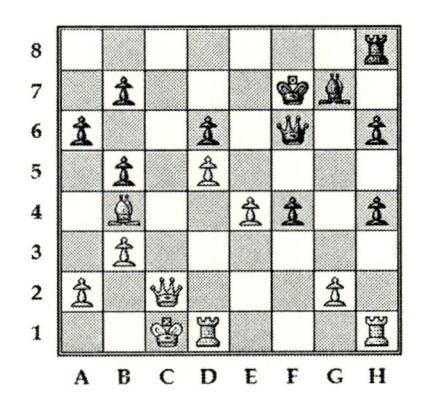

If only the white queen could be decoyed from protecting the b2 square, The Restless Knight would have checkmate!

26...Rc8! 27.Kd2 [27.Qxc8 Qb2#]

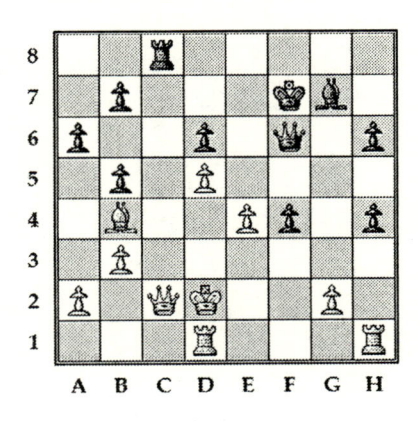

The Great Pawn Hunter - 138

27...Rxc2+ 28.Kxc2 Qb2+ 29.Kd3 Qd4+ 30.Ke2 Qxb4 31.Kf3

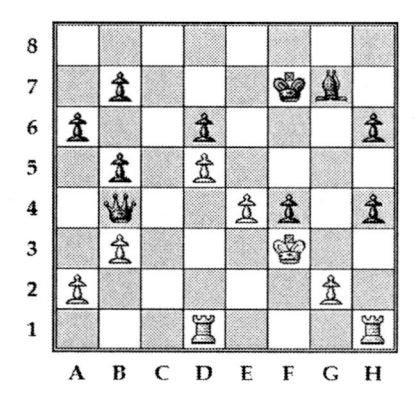

The Talker desperately flees to the kingside.

31...Qc3+ 32.Ke2 Qe3+ 33.Kf1 f3

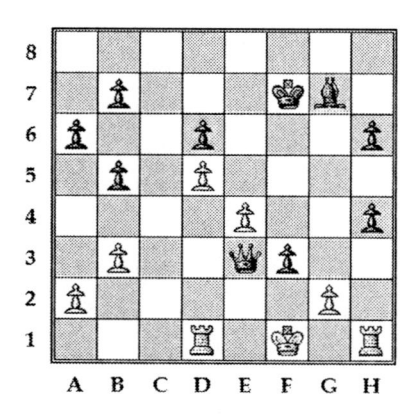

[33...f3 34.Re1 (34.gxf3 Qxf3+! ; 34.Rh2) 34...fxg2+ 35.Kxg2 Qg3+ 36.Kf1 Qf3+ 37.Kg1 Bd4+ 38.Re3 Bxe3+ 39.Kh2 Qg3#] 0-1

Yes, my friends, that day the villain was vanquished yet again and the eagle soared on a summits peak to the delight of the good guys.

Game
Zschaebitz,K (2176) - Dworakowska,J (2350) [A80]
Lasker mem op Barlinek (1), 16.07.2001

The Mountain Heights
A poem

There is no love in badness.
It only brings one sadness.
On the mountain heights
or the valley's low,
it's God that reigns
not an evil foe.
Only love
can bring us
gladness.
So, let your hearts
be merry
and tip a glass
or two
and say with me
these simple words
"Dear friend,
I love you"

The Great Pawn Hunter

The Intrepid Warrior

The Intrepid Warrior put his ear to the ground. "He's near," said he. "Yes, yes, he's very near." He gathered some grass, from the side of the road, into his palm. Then, he counted off 64 steps and launched the grass into the air...

Now, it was all about noon in the middle of a hot sunny day. The Great Pawn Hunter was sitting on the steps of his porch sipping a glass of lemonade and basking in the sunshine. Now, days like this were few and far between. Most days, he had chores to do. But, today was his and he was enjoying every second of it for as long as it lasted. Now, you know as well as I, it never lasts long. He went to place his chess pieces onto his chess mat that he had put on the porch and discovered he was missing a bishop. He searched high and low but to no avail. "Well," said he "this is not going to ruin my bright sunny day." "But," he confessed "it does bring a cloud or two." So, in the place of the bishop he put a pebble.
He went into the house and emerged with a newspaper. He opened it and turned to the chess section. He was calculating a move variation when the wind picked up and ruffled his newspaper. He glanced up and looked around. He didn't see a thing. But, a feeling went through him. He only got this feeling when he sat down to play...a "rated" game of chess. "A challenge?" he thought, but from who and from where? ...

Studiously, the Intrepid Warrior analyzed the wind current. Its ever-changing course would lead him onward. "South, West, North, East! Yes, East! Oh, he's near. He's very, very near." said he and off he went repeating his calculating method every sixty four steps...

Meanwhile, The Great Pawn Hunter gazed around him. He noticed a small figure running towards him at full stride and shouting something. As she made her way up to him, The Great Pawn Hunter said, "Hi, Restless. Do you want to play a game of " However, The Restless Knight grabbed his hand and pulled it towards her and said urgently, "Quick you must come and see this!" Well, before they could go off the porch, they noticed a man, dressed in black, crossing at the top of their street. In the middle of the road, he stooped. He put his ear to the ground and launched something into the air. He paused for a calculating moment and...turned in their direction...

"Who do you think he is?" asked The Great Pawn Hunter. The Restless Knight replied in a whisper "Shhhh! Count." "Count of what?" whispered The Great Pawn Hunter. The Restless Knight whispered, "His footsteps. Count his footsteps."

Now, the Intrepid Warrior was finishing his steps and The Great Pawn Hunter was finishing his count "sixty two, sixty three, sixty four!" when the Intrepid Warrior stopped right in front of The Great Pawn Hunter's porch. The Great Pawn Hunter had come face to face with a puzzling enigma. The two chess players gazed, in curiosity, down at the mysterious person. The Intrepid Warrior put his ear to the ground. Then he got up and threw some grass into the air. Well,

The Great Pawn Hunter - 143

the grass went straight up and then came straight down landing all over him. "He's here! I've found him!" shouted the Intrepid Warrior to the air. The Restless Knight smiled and asked the Intrepid Warrior, "Who's here?" The Intrepid Warrior looked up at her from the road and out came his words "My king, my king is here." The Great Pawn Hunter sat motionless. The Intrepid Warrior's words had reached the very fiber of The Great Pawn Hunter's being. For when The Great Pawn Hunter played chess...he was the king!

"Would you like to play a game of chess?" asked The Great Pawn Hunter to the Intrepid Warrior. The Intrepid Warrior walked up three steps to the landing of The Great Pawn Hunter's porch. He gazed at the pebble, in the place of where the bishop was, and asked The Great Pawn Hunter, "Do you miss it?" The Great Pawn Hunter replied, "Desperately!" The Intrepid Warrior smiled and said, "Yes, I'll play for you." Well, they played their game of chess and the two chess players fought valiantly.
1.e4 c5 Sicilian Defense.

The Great Pawn Hunter - 144

2.Nf3 d6 3.d4 cxd4 4.Nxd4 Nf6 5.Nc3 a6 6.Bg5 e6 7.f4 Qb6 8.Nb3 Nbd7 9.Qf3 Qc7 10.0-0-0 b5

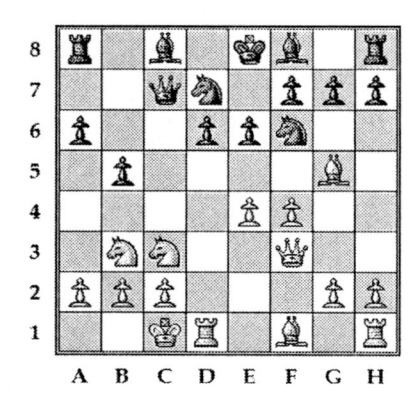

threatening to kick the c3 knight from protecting the e4 pawn.

11.Bd3 Bb7 12.a3 (stopping b4.)
12 ..., Be7 13.Rhe1

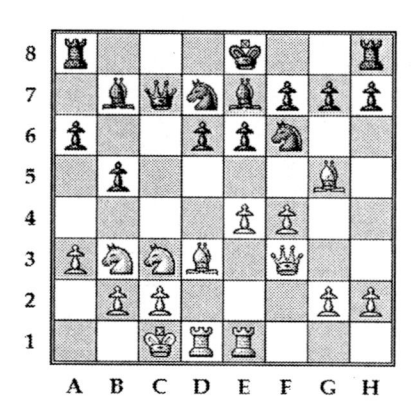

The Great Pawn Hunter centralizes his last white piece. Now for the attack!

13...0-0-0 14.f5 Rhe8 15.fxe6 fxe6

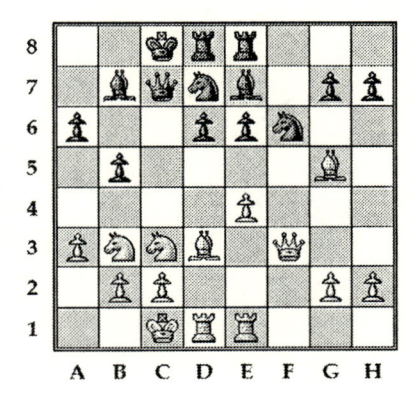

The Great Pawn Hunter has created three black pawn islands and he wastes no time in attacking them with Qh3!

16.Qh3 Bf8 17.Nd4 Nc5 18.Nd5

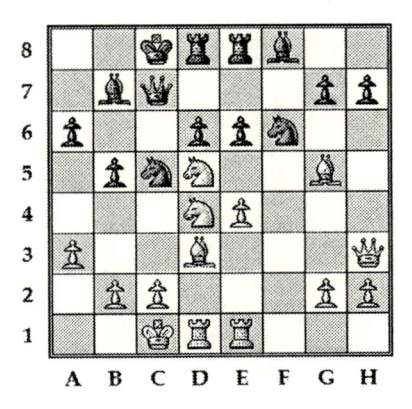

The Great Pawn Hunter - 146

The d5 square is now weakened. All this was because of the pin by The Great Pawn Hunter's queen.

18...Nxd5 19.exd5 Bxd5 20.Bxd8

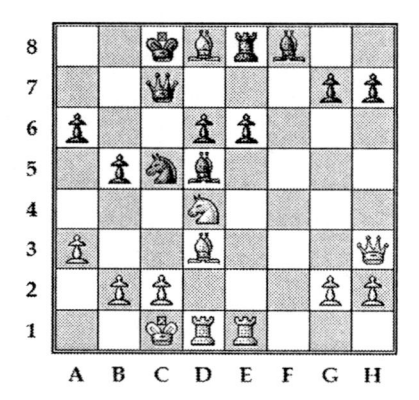

The Intrepid Warrior could only watch in amazement as The Great Pawn Hunter marshaled his troops.

20...Qxd8 21.Kb1 Kb8 22.Bxh7

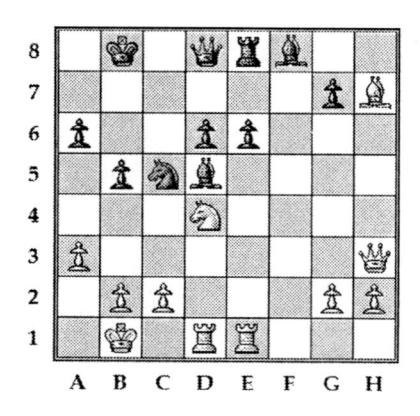

Another bishop gets into the act.

22...Be7 23.Qh5 Kb7 24.Nf5 Kc6 25.Rxd5 exd5

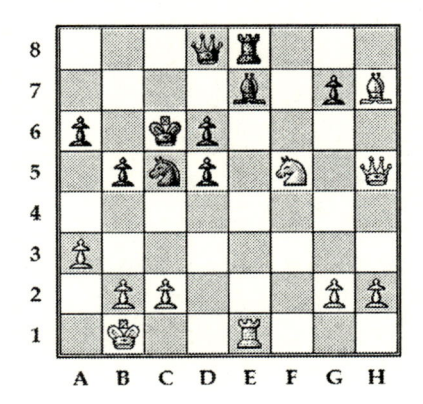

Studying the subtle pinning imbalances, The Great Pawn Hunter finishes it off with a simple bishop move, tipping the scales.

26.Bg6

The Intrepid Warrior extended his hand for a handshake in humble gratitude for a game well played. 1-0
When the game was over, the Intrepid Warrior asked The Great Pawn Hunter and The Restless Knight for a cup of lemonade. They went into the house and returned with the glass only to discover the Intrepid Warrior had left the premises. The chess players never did discover where he went ...or had they? For on The Great Pawn Hunter's chessboard, the pebble had been replaced with a beautiful intrepid bishop. Now you know who the Intrepid Warrior was all along

and where he disappeared to. I hope you keep his secret just between you and me.

Game
Pavlovic,M (2500) - Roschina,T (2322) [B97]
Biel MTO Biel (2), 24.07.2001

Itty Bitty
Ain't She So Pretty
Little Kitty Blues
A poem

That feline has been here,
hasn't she?

Yes Whiskey, I'm afraid she has.

She has marked even my owner.
A tough pill to swallow.

Oh Whiskey, I hope you can
take this.
You're a big kitty now.
She's sweet. You could learn
a lot from her.

Well, she's not going
to get her paw prints
on me.
First the cuddle,
then the cold shoulder.
Let Meowt!
I've got to get out.
I'm going to visit a true friend.
There's a place up the street
where all the cool cat's meet.
A shoulder to cry on
a paw to lend.
And its steeple rises high,
way up to the sky.
When you're up there,
the world never ends.

The Great Pawn Hunter - 150

Well, Whiskey, I don't mean
to interrupt you my friend.
I think it's safe to say
you've got the
Itty Bitty "Ain't she so Pretty"
Little Kitty Blues.
I can see you are stressed.
That feline's got you depressed.
That's how they make
you pay
your dues!
But meows can't erase
a sweet paw in the face
or her warm cuddle
underneath a wet porch.
You're not fooling me
Whiskey I can see,
my friend, the light
of your torch.
Whiskey, Where are you going?

Let meowt!
I've got to get out.
I'm going to visit a true friend.
There's a place up the street
where all the cool cat's meet.
A shoulder to cry on
a paw to lend.
And its steeple rises high,
way up to the sky.
When you're up there,
the world never ends.

Whiskey, my friend,
It's not the end.
On the contrary,

it could be a start.
Once bitten, twice shy.
My friend, that's no lie.
Be careful who you give
your heart.
When you're up there today,
a prayer you could say,
one for me and one for you.
Because, your owner's been
so very there, filled with despair
down and out, down and blue.
And, I went up there, with all my despair,
looking for God, a Few Friends.
Just as when I was young,
and I was brought up
to that steeple high in the air
and the priest let me look out
to see where the world stops.
Whiskey: the world never ends.

And from then to today
the world spins away
and his feline has marked
all his spots
But, Whiskey's purring away.
I guess you could say
"For her,
he still has the hots!"

The Great Pawn Hunter

The Wisdom of Solomon

My friends, this writing is not only meant to entertain you with a chapter from the life of The Talker. It is a story about love and justice. You see, The Talker's coldness all stemmed from growing up alone without love from anyone to nudge him in the right direction. However, with a few kind words, in the proper environment, a person, yes even The Talker, can be happy and at peace. Isn't that what it is all about? So, with that in mind, let us begin our story...

It was a dreary, drizzly day in the great city. The Talker couldn't find an opponent, unlucky enough, for him to exert his will over. "There's not a game to be had in this tumbleweed town," said The Talker to himself. He would have to be content with only reading about chess in the chess section of the newspaper.

He opened the paper and started reading when, on about the third paragraph down, he saw an advertisement that talked about the latest computer game for chess. Now, The Great Pawn Hunter and The Restless Knight used computer chess games as sparring partners to hone their skills. However, that is not what The Talker had in mind. No, he saw a floundering fish. One that could not jump or swim away. A fish made to fry and seasoned to taste. He cut out the advertisement from the paper and ran to the computer store. Little did he know that the computer game could be warmer and more forgiving than he.

By the time he arrived in the store, it was raining out. He landed in the software aisle soaked to the skin. A lightning bolt lit up the sky outside as he searched through the software titles. He looked on the top shelf and then on the bottom shelf. However, he couldn't find the computer chess game he was looking for. So, he went to Fritz, the manager on duty. Now, Fritz was busy pricing software in another aisle, with his pricing gun, when The Talker found him and asked the big question. "Fritz, do you have any chess software?" Well, the good natured manager put down his pricing gun and went off to see if he had software that The Talker could afford. Fritz checked and double checked. However, he found he was all sold out of it. So, The Talker searched for other computer games to entertain his diabolical mind.

There was "Caissa's Knight, Wrath of the Castle". This was a computer game that The Talker had mastered long ago. In the hands of The Talker, the villain had made a pawn out of the computerized hero. Talented? Yes, he was...in a diabolical way. Then, there was the thriller software "Eating the Rhino." The Talker smiled a mischievous smile. "Been there, done that," said The Talker to himself. Finally, he came to a computer chess game that had three syllables and a king on the cover. The name of the chess game was Solomon. "Hmmm" thought The Talker. "Fritz must have made a mistake. What a loser!" said The Talker to himself. Now, coming from The Talker, that was a high compliment. For, due to his upbringing, he couldn't say a kind word to save his life. So, The Talker spent an extra few minutes to diabolically mix up all the software titles on the shelves. He put "Eating the Rhino" in with the cooking software. He put "Caissa's Knight" in with the sports games. Then he triumphantly lowered the pricing on many of his other favorite computer games for he had Fritz's pricing gun. "A job well done," said he, "I'll be back."

Well, he went to the check out line and purchased the chess game with milk money he got from students, in shady dealings, at school lunch break, which, by the way, was just after math class. Yes folks, a cold calculating capitalist. In other words ... a scoundrel!

He got home and installed the computer game onto his computer. He quickly clicked on the icon to start a game. However, before he could play, Solomon asked him to choose a computerized person to play against. Solomon had many computerized chess players to pick from and The Talker was to pick only one. Ironically, his decision was...a friendly opponent.
Mind you, friendship was not on The Talker's mind. Over the years, he had become enclosed in his own little world. If no one wanted to play with him he would find his own fun and that was just fine with him. Well folks, friendship was not on the computer's mind either. You might say this chess game was made for him. For when the computer acknowledged the opponent that The Talker had chosen, it left the "r" out of "friendly." Folks, The Talker was going to face a fiendly opponent!

The game began. After The Talker made his first move, thunder roared outside his window and then Solomon made its move. Imagine the shock The Talker must have felt when Solomon replied to The

The Great Pawn Hunter - 155

Talker's move with human speech: "I'm going to crush you like a grape!" said Solomon and the thunder roared once more. Now, this made The Talker jump and he ran out of the room. But, in a few seconds, he composed himself. After all it was only a computer. But, he did admit it was scary to have the computer talk back to him, especially since, those were the very words The Talker said to his opponents. In the game that was played, The Talker had the white pieces and Solomon had the black:

1.e4 e5 2.f4 King's Gambit

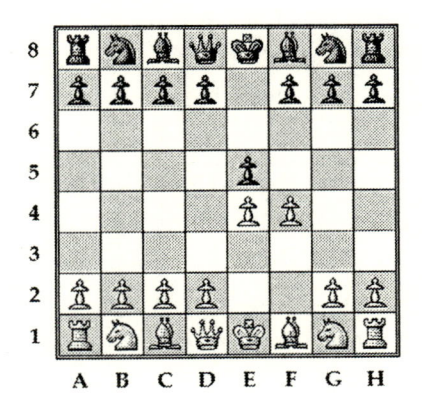

2...Bc5 3.Nf3 d6 4.b4 Bb6 5.Bb2 Nf6 6.fxe5 dxe5 7.Bxe5 0-0 8.Bxf6 Qxf6 9.e5 Qf4 10.d4 Bg4 11.c3 Bxf3 12.gxf3 Nc6 13.Qd2 Qh4+ 14.Kd1 Rad8 15.Kc2

The Great Pawn Hunter - 156

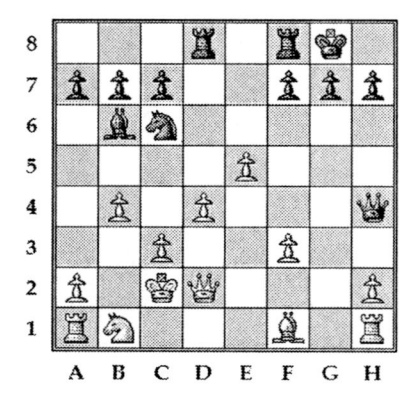

Now Solomon destroys The Talker's pawn cover around his white king.

15...Bxd4 16.cxd4 Nxd4+

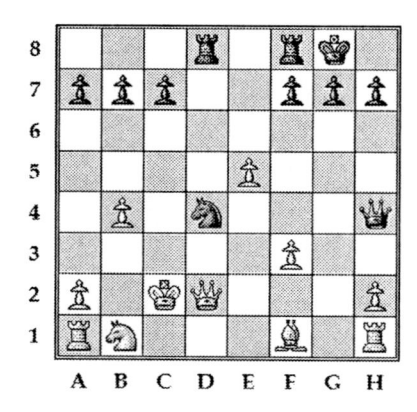

Black threatens a devious discovered double attack against the white queen and the b4 pawn.

17.Kb2 Nb5 18.Qe3 Qxb4+ 19.Kc1 Rd5 20.Bxb5

Desperately trying to reduce the number of attackers.

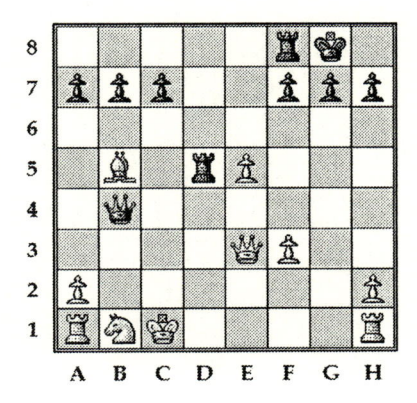

20...Rxb5 21.Qd2 Rc5+ the black rooks and queen have too many open avenues.

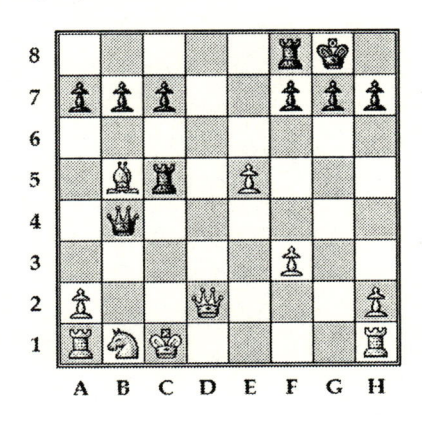

22.Kd1 Qa4+ 23.Ke1 Qh4+ 24.Ke2 Rxe5+ Solomon's pieces have complete harmony.

The Great Pawn Hunter - 158

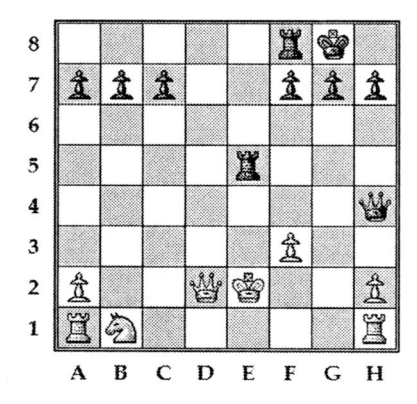

25.Kf1 Rd8 26.Qc1 Qd4 27.Qxc7 Qd3+ 28.Kf2 Re2+ 29.Kg3

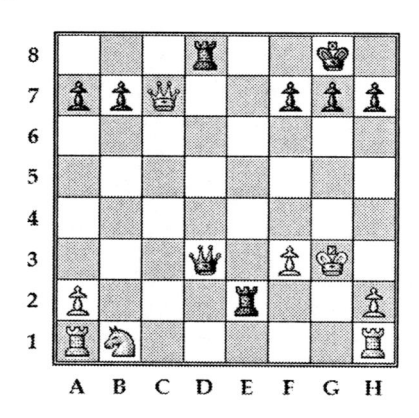

The king clings to his lowly pawn but "one pawn does not a king shield."

29...Qg6+ 30.Kh4 Qh6+ 31.Kg4 Rd4+ 32.f4 Rg2+ 33.Kf5 Qe6# 0-1

The Great Pawn Hunter - 159

Well, The Talker was phased only a little. His will was still strong. One thing he had learned from playing chess was not to give up that easily and he started another game. But, he was so nervous that, by some act of heaven, he hit a key on the computer's keyboard that put Solomon into "training mode".

The Talker cautiously moved a piece and the computer responded with another phrase, but a much warmer one. "Oh, I wouldn't move there," said Solomon. "Trust me" it said. The Talker wouldn't take back the move. Solomon replied "If you move there you will lose a piece my friend." and it showed The Talker the reason why. Well, The Talker was not completely lost. For The Talker took back his move and pushed another piece. I guess he just needed someone to explain things to him. Don't we all.

Now, Solomon wasn't done with his kind words and uplifting remarks. "That's better," said Solomon in a different voice, "it is good you listened to us." Yes, the computer said "Us!" For, The Talker was not facing one computerized opponent. He was playing with all of Solomon's computerized players with language and playing styles from all over the world and all at the same time. "Wonderful," you say...Yes, wonderful it was, for The Talker had found a warm slightly buggy world to play in and opponent's he couldn't hurt.

Was this a chink in Solomon's armor? Had the programmers that created it made a ghastly mistake? We'll never know. All I know is this, with every move there came a new personality. With every new personality, there came a different computerized plan and each plan was conflicting with the other. When all was said and done, it was The Talker that emerged happy and victorious. Yes my friends, he became a much more trusting and well adjusted scoundrel, although, a thoroughly mixed up and completely confused one and that my friends is love and justice and that is as it should be.

Game
Berg,E (2474) - Hector,J (2546) [C30]
SWE-ch Linkoping (6), 05.07.2001

Honey from a Bee
A poem

Why do we turn out
the way we are?
Was there love in our life
when we look back afar?
Now, even the flowers
are loved by the bees.
Honey, a gift from above
and a home in the trees.
Now, someone is fighting
while I'm writing this poem.
There's no love in their heart.
There's no safety or warmth.
So, why do I mention
this unpeaceful event?
It's why we were born.
It's why we were sent.
To grow with each other.
To bring love to today.
It took long to get there.
It's what I wanted to say.
So, this poem began with
honey from a bee.
Yes, God brings me to you
and He brings you to me
and He caresses us all
with love, sweet and free.

The Great Pawn Hunter

A Teacup Full of Steam

As the sun stood ground on the horizon, the clock ticked and the kettle roared for attention. It was morning. The Restless Knight was writing a poem at The Great Pawn Hunter's kitchen table. She reached over and gave the knob on the stove a twist. The kettle's roar faded into a whisper. The steam from the kettle rose and the teacup was filled, soon to be adorned with lemon and honey. This is just what The Restless Knight needed to start her poem off on a good note. However, a bad feeling came over her. She looked around her. She could see The Great Pawn Hunter, in the living room, watching one of his favorite programs on the television. It was the courtroom channel and he was sitting enjoying a brisk cup of ...tea!

Now, there are a million and one reasons not to have a good day in this world. It seemed that The Restless Knight had gone through a million of them in only a week. As bad luck would have it, The Restless Knight opened the doors to the kitchen cabinet to discover The Great Pawn Hunter had used the last bit of honey in the house. She scrambled to the refrigerator and pulled open its doors and searched in vain for the lemon was gone too!

Well, on the courtroom channel, the jury had reached their verdict. "What say you?" said the judge to the jury "Is he guilty or innocent?" The Restless Knight's thoughts gelled into one all encompassing verdict "Lemon is bitter. He's as guilty as sin. You'll find the evidence in his teacup and dribbling from his chin!" What a time for a poem to occur in the heat of

The Great Pawn Hunter - 163

vengeance and all. The Great Pawn Hunter got up from his chair and came into the kitchen. The Restless Knight asked The Great Pawn Hunter if the villain had been convicted. The Great Pawn Hunter replied "Restless, it was bittersweet. They settled for a lesser crime and a shorter sentence."

Now, just then the doorbell rang and a shudder went through The Great Pawn Hunter's body. The dog was barking uncontrollably. The mail had arrived. The Restless Knight, being kind as she always is, went to retrieve the mail for The Great Pawn Hunter. But, today was to be a day altogether different. It was reason one million and one! "Lesser crime?" thought The Restless Knight. "He finished the last bit of honey!" She opened the door to greet the mailman when out popped a comment The Restless Knight had no means of controlling. It had built up inside of her. The volcano erupted and so she yelled "Throw the book at him, I say!" My friends, I guess, sometimes, you just have to let it all out.

Now the mailman was surprised. For, along with countless bills, the mailman had a book to deliver. "Throw it at whom?" asked the mailman. "Ya know, I'm quite a good aim." said he and he smiled a disarming smile. The Restless Knight replied "I was just yelling to myself." "Oh," said the mailman "did I ring the doorbell to loudly?" After reflecting on The Great Pawn Hunter's reaction to the bell, Restless replied "No, you rang it just perfectly,...but you could ring it a little louder next time."
Well, the mailman left the porch to complete his rounds. The Restless Knight brought the mail to The Great Pawn Hunter. There were more late notices for The Great Pawn Hunter's family than you could

shake a stick at. The Restless Knight realized that The Great Pawn Hunter needed a bit of honey in his life too. She felt sorry for feeling so angry. She looked through the coupon book. In it there were coupons to all the stores and eating establishments in the area and one of these was "Castle French Fry" a fast food place and local chess player haven. It was well known that if your chess game was poor, and you needed a tour, you could find fish all the more at The Castle.

So, The Restless Knight searched through her pockets. All she had on her was enough to buy two dinners without the soda. "There is never a discount on soda!" thought Restless. "There ought to be a law." She couldn't even afford a cup of tea. However, her mind started churning. "Hmmm," said she "with a fish dinner you get lemon!" Ahhh to see her mind in motion was a thing of beauty as was she. "And, with chicken nuggets you get a honey dipping sauce...Hmmm!"

Then it hit her like a bolt out of the blue. She boiled some water and put it in a thermos. Next, she added a couple of tea bags to steep and closed the lid. She walked over to The Great Pawn Hunter and rested her hand on his shoulder. "Great Pawn Hunter," said Restless, "get up from your seat. For, you've got a treat. Keep your money in your pocket's 'cause we're going out to eat." And, the two French Fry companions left the house to the dog and the bills as they made their way up the street and turned the corner.

Now, at The Castle they played the following game. All gathered around the table to see the chess players having fun. The Restless Knight played the black pieces and The Great Pawn Hunter played the white pieces.

1.e4 c5 Sicilian Defense

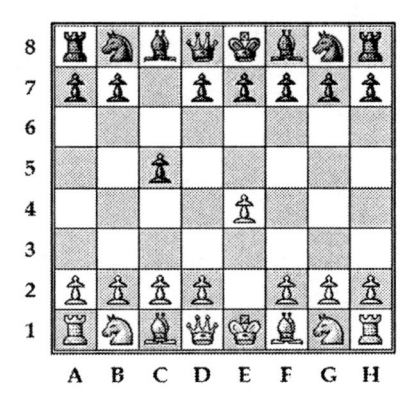

2.Nf3 d6 3.d4 cxd4 4.Nxd4 Nf6 5.Nc3 a6 Najdorf Variation.

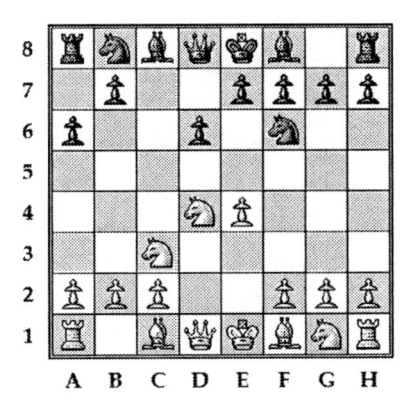

The Great Pawn Hunter - 166

6.Be2 e5 7.Nb3 Be7 8.0-0 0-0 9.Kh1 Bd7 10.Be3 Bc6 11.Bf3 Nbd7 12.a4 b6 13.Qd3 Bb7 14.h3 Rc8 15.Rad1 h6 16.Rfe1 Qc7 17.g3 Rfd8 18.Kh2 Re8 19.Re2 Qc4

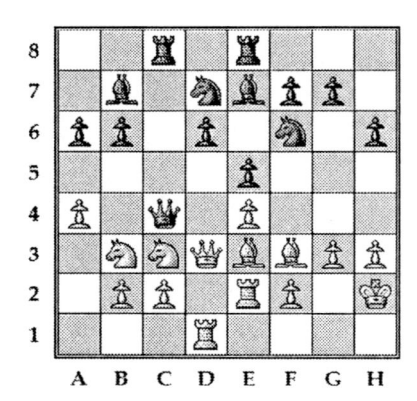

The Restless Knight offers to trades queens to decrease The Great Pawn Hunter's tactical ability.

20.Qxc4 Rxc4 21.Nd2 Rc7 22.Bg2 Rec8 23.Nb3

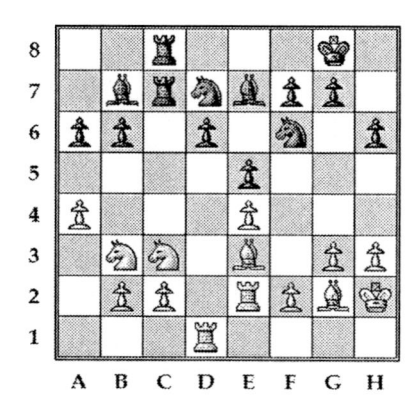

The Great Pawn Hunter - 167

The e pawn will fall only if the c3 knight is removed. The Restless Knight doesn't blink. She sacrifices the rook and offers a stunning draw.

23...Rxc3 24.bxc3 Bxe4 25.Bc1

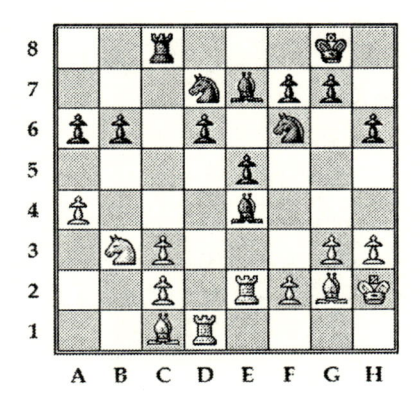

The Great Pawn Hunter shows his mobility by bringing the bishop around to a3 with a threat on the backward d pawn.

25...Bxg2 26.Kxg2 Rxc3 27.Ba3 Ne8 28.f4

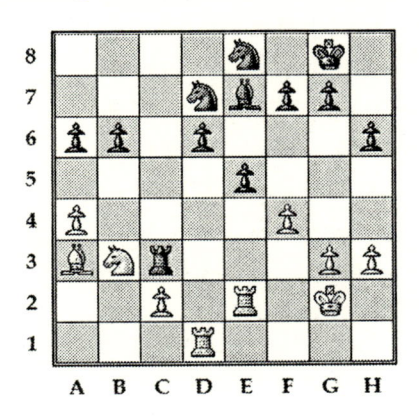

Then, with friendship in heart, The Great Pawn Hunter decides to accept her offer of a draw and go home as friends. 1/2-1/2

Game
DEEP JUNIOR - Kasparov,G (2847) [B92]
FIDE Man-Machine WC New York USA (6), 07.02.2003

Steam
A poem

When the steam builds up
inside you
and your temper is
in doubt.
Don't hold it all
inside you.
You've got to
let it out.
For Friendship is
something special.
So, keep this all
in hand.
Water is simply
wetter
than a desert
full of
sand.

The Great Pawn Hunter

Elusive and Free

The Sun glistened on the river and magnified its murky depths. Was it a log or was it a fish? I'll tell you now, my friends, it was no bigger than a twig. The Great Pawn Hunter waited until this shadow, moving just below the surface of the water, drifted down stream to a shallow pocket. He reached into his tackle box and found his lure, a beautiful bumble bee made out of pillow feathers, brown and yellow yarn. He masterfully cast his homemade lure upstream and let it drift, guiding it ever carefully with the precision of an experienced fisherman. The lure hit the pocket and was caught by the shadowy figure. The Great Pawn Hunter raised his fishing rod violently and set the hook into this murky shadowy monster of a fish!

Yes, The Great Pawn Hunter had dreams of a mighty fish that would leap in defiance so he set the hook accordingly. However, the fish kept going about its duties being a fish. And, to The Great Pawn Hunter, a very big one at that. Well, The Great Pawn Hunter's heart was palpitating. He kept the fishing rod high in the air, as Old Maestro had taught him years before, and watched as the shadow drifted out of the shallow pocket and into the current. All the while, it dragged the line out of The Great Pawn Hunter's fishing reel.

The Great Pawn Hunter had second thoughts "Maybe it's not a fish. Maybe it's a log. After all, I didn't actually see the fish." My friends, all he saw was a shadow. But, logs don't swim to the other side of the river, as this log was doing right about now.

Well, the fishing line started to make a "Tinging" sound. The kind of sound it makes just before it snaps. The Great Pawn Hunter knew it was the last stand. It was catch this fish or go home empty handed.

Suddenly, the line was pulling the fishing rod from him. However, The Great Pawn Hunter stood ground and held on firm. Gradually, though, his feet went into the water. Then, his knees went in. Soon, he was waist-deep in the current. However, he wouldn't let go! Well, the water raged around him. He would have been swept away, but, he held on firm to that fishing rod and, at the end of the line, the fish!

He was neck-high in river water when he had a fleeting thought, "If the fish lets go, I'll surely be drowned!" But the fish didn't let go. He just swam his fishy tail upstream and dragged The Great Pawn Hunter behind him, boots, fly rod and all. Imagine seeing a fisherman being dragged upstream by a fish the size of a twig...a ghastly sight, yes. Nevertheless, the sun surely shines.

Well, The Great Pawn Hunter's heart was beating even louder as he frantically reeled in the line, ever inching his way towards that puzzling fish. The Great Pawn Hunter would catch him with his bare hands if he had to, that is, if this evasive fish would let him. If only he could catch a glimpse of his watery foe, he would die a happy fisherman. The Great Pawn Hunter got to within one foot of the fish and plunged his head underneath the water. There before him he saw the cause of his curious adventure, a beautiful rainbow trout about a twig's length in size.

The Great Pawn Hunter made a lunge for the trout but the trout spit The Great Pawn Hunter's homemade bumble bee back at him. The trout was free and so was the bee. The Great Pawn Hunter reached for his homemade lure and it caught in his finger. Well, if you could scream under water it would sound much like The Great Pawn Hunter, with a few bubbles added, as he watched the rainbow trout get smaller and smaller for The Great Pawn Hunter was now being washed away with the current.

The Great Pawn Hunter floated safely down to a small island of rocks jutting out of the middle of the river. It was there he washed up upon its rocky banks, as if the fish had planned it. It was there that The Restless Knight found him in a row boat. He was empty handed, except for the vision of a beautiful rainbow and the gentle smile of a trusting and caring friend.

Now, after drying out a while and trading fish stories, they realized they were in the middle of the river on a rocky island with no one to bug them but a small fish leaping for flies off in the distance. Well, at least The Great Pawn Hunter had The Restless Knight to protect him. Restless took out her magnetic chess set and the two chess players played the following game of chess in solitude. The Great Pawn Hunter played the white pieces and The Restless Knight played black:

The Great Pawn Hunter - 173

1.e4 e6 French Defense

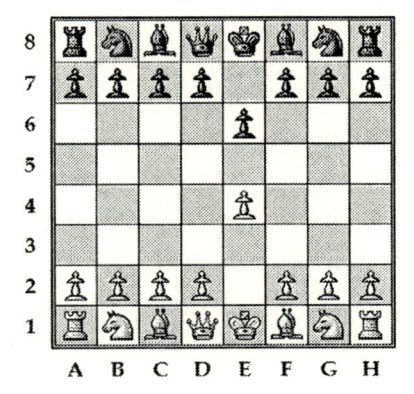

2.d4 d5 3.Nc3 Nf6 4.e5 Nfd7 Steinitz Variation

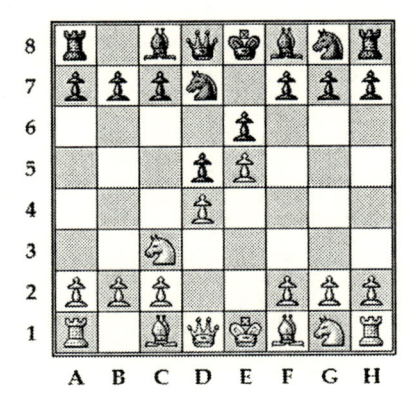

5.Nce2 c5 6.c3 Nc6 7.Nf3 cxd4 8.cxd4 Be7 9.g3 0-0 10.Bg2 b6 11.0-0 Ba6 12.Re1 Bxe2 13.Rxe2 b5 14.h4 Qb6 15.Bg5

The Great Pawn Hunter - 174

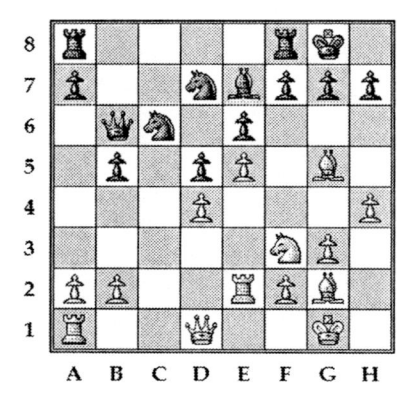

The Great Pawn Hunter offers to trade his bad white bishop for The Restless Knight's good black bishop.

15...Bxg5 16.hxg5 Rfc8 17.Bf1 a5 18.Rd2 Nf8 19.Kg2 g6

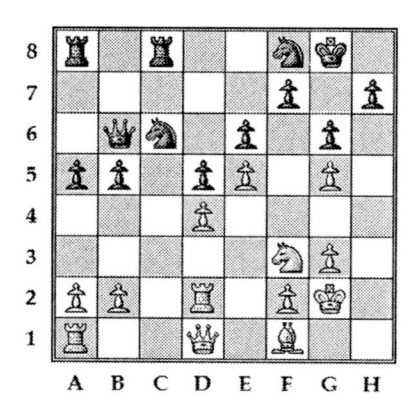

The Restless Knight makes a fatal mistake, creating pawn holes on f6 and h6.

20.Nh2 Nd7 21.Ng4 Na7 22.Qf3 Kg7 23.Bd3

The Great Pawn Hunter - 175

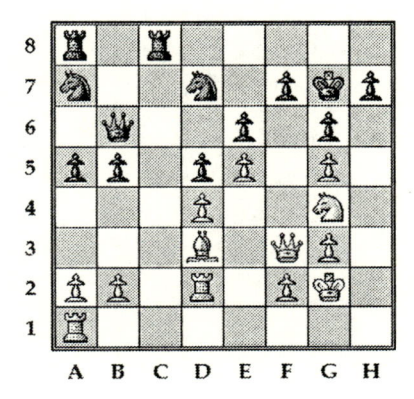

With the center closed, The Great Pawn Hunter's army rushes to the kingside for the attack.

23...Nc6 24.Rh1 Rh8 25.Nh6 Rhf8

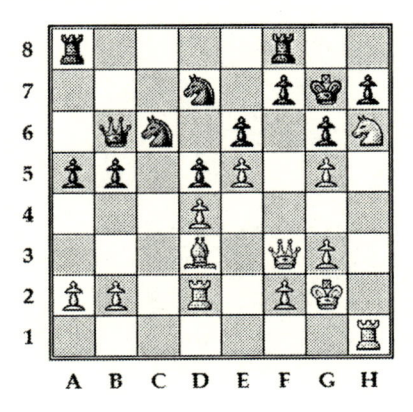

26.Nxf7! Nd8 27.Rxh7+ Kxh7

The pawn structure surrounding the black king is demolished.

The Great Pawn Hunter - 176

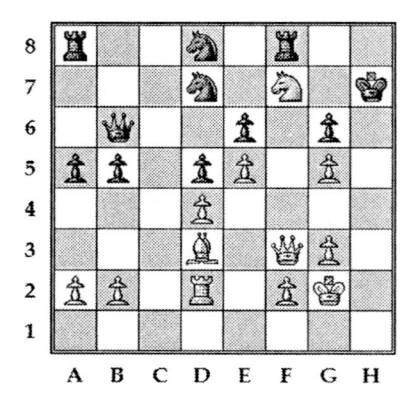

The pin on the g6 pawn spells doom. The pawn no longer protects the h5 square and this allows the white queen to join the attack.

28.Qh5+ [28.Qh5+ Kg7 29.Qxg6#] 1-0

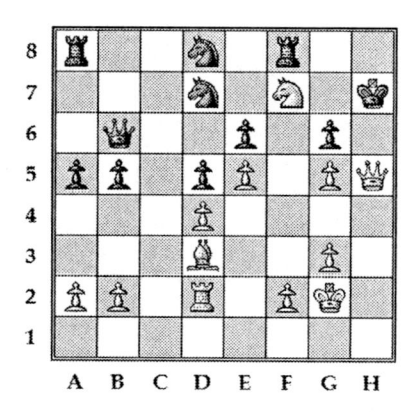

My friends, to me, God is like that fish, elusive and free. We try to catch Him but it is Him catching us. We go through troubled waters. But, if we keep focused on Him, we just might see that beautiful rainbow, a wonderful creation like The Great Pawn Hunter's attack in the chess game above.

Game
Paschall,W (2332) - Kessler,H [C11]
Bayern-chI Bank Hofmann 3rd Bad Wiessee (1), 23.10.1999

A Whale of A Fish
A poem

A fish has a tail.
So does a whale.
It swings it
like thunder
as big as a sail.
Though, it's as big
as a house,
It's as gentle
as a mouse
and you can't
fit that fish
in a pail.

The Great Pawn Hunter

The Rusty Old Gate

Outside the school, the birds were chirping and a chess player was planting flowers. Another was scraping a rusty old entrance gate to the detention hall for troublemakers. My friends, it was The Great Pawn Hunter, in the thick of it, and here is his story...

It was the last day of March. The Talker was busy at the teacher's desk, studying for the surprise mathematics quiz which was held every Tuesday, tomorrow to be precise. The Great Pawn Hunter and The Restless Knight were at Castle French Fry, their favorite place to eat, meet friends and play chess. Now The Restless Knight was eating a healthy salad. She couldn't help but glance over and see The Great Pawn Hunter eat his messy, greasy, slimy hamburger. "Great Pawn Hunter," said Restless, "have you ever thought of being a vegetarian?" The Great Pawn Hunter looked at her and then at his food. Then, with a sudden role of the eyes, like a great white shark before it devours its prey, The Great Pawn Hunter took a bite out of his hamburger. Her question didn't phase him a bit. He just answered her, half chewing and sipping his soda at the same time. "I am a vegetarian!" said he with a glug, glug and a slurp.

Well, The Restless Knight was confused to say the least. "What do you mean you're a vegetarian? You are eating a hamburger. Doesn't that come from a cow?" said she. The Great Pawn Hunter replied, "I am a vegetarian by mathematics!" Well, The Restless Knight had to see this through to its ultimate conclusion...that The Great Pawn Hunter had flipped his lid, and was crazy as a loon. For, not all of his eggs were surely in the same basket.

The Great Pawn Hunter continued with his unerring line of reasoning. "Have you ever heard of the Mathematical Law of Association?" asked he. The Restless Knight smiled a perplexed smile and raised her eyebrow "Yes, go on," said she. The Restless Knight couldn't wait to hear this one. "Well," said The Great Pawn Hunter "the law states 'if (A equals B) and (B equals C) then (A equals C).' Am I right?" said he. "So far, go on" said she. "Now, if I eat the cow and the cow eats the plants then I am eating the plants too. Therefore, I am a vegetarian by association," said The Great Pawn Hunter "Ladies and gentlemen of the jury, " said he to the air around him, "I rest my case." and he took another bite of his hamburger. The Restless Knight said to her self , "I was right he has lost it." "You can't argue with facts Restless," said The Great Pawn Hunter, "It's a law of science. Do you want a bite?" and he took a sip of his soda. Now, Restless weighed her reply carefully. But, quite frankly, she thought, "One of the bubbles in his soda went straight to his brain!" However, she replied skirting the obvious, "I'll have a French fry." said she. My friends, he pushed over his carton of French fries.

Well, the next day came, April Fool's Day, and the bell for homeroom ended. It was time for the mathematics test. The teacher passed out the tests and asked the students to pass them over their heads to the ones behind them. All the students sat with butterflies in their stomachs, except for The Great Pawn Hunter who knew his subject well, and The Talker who, for some curious reason, didn't, but he didn't seem to care. The Talker had his mind on other things. "Plotting and planning is all in a days work. It's too much for one scoundrel to take. But, I'll handle it!" thought he to himself.

As The Great Pawn Hunter passed back the tests, he looked around the classroom. He saw The Restless Knight in the first row. Gradually, he looked down to the back row where he saw The Talker smiling back at him, and it was a mischievous smile at that. This unnerved The Great Pawn Hunter, something was up. He looked back at The Talker a second time. The Talker was chewing bubble gum. He stretched some from his teeth and put it back in his mouth without the teacher seeing him do it, for he was in stealth mode.

Well, The Great Pawn Hunter kept his gum in his desk. He got an uneasy feeling. "Maybe, The Talker is chewing my bubble gum!" thought he. So, he lifted the lid of his desk and peeked inside. But, what he saw was an opened mathematics book. He tried to close the lid of his desk and noticed two feet next to him. He looked up. It was the teacher. Her name was Louise but the students called her "Big Louie." She opened the cover of his desk and there before her was the mathematics book turned to the page that the test was on.

Well, Big Louie was 6 feet tall and had a grin that could scare a rhinoceros. She had teeth so big she could bite your head off in one chomp. She picked up his book and ripped it in two with the strength of a woolly mammoth! Then, she took The Great Pawn Hunter by the ear and ushered The Great Pawn Hunter out of the room to the principal's office. From there, he found he was sentenced to serve two weeks of detention. Now, my friends, where's the love? I say, where's the love in that?

Well, he walked through that rusty old gate of detention hall, up the steps and through the doors. He entered the room, where the monitor was on duty, ready to punish The Great Pawn Hunter, alias 'Prisoner 1803'. Now, the classroom monitor, "Sarge" as the prisoners called him, was an ex-marine. He liked to write poetry, read his bible, and play chess. However, because of his size, rumors were spread that he ate students for breakfast! Sarge pointed to where The Great Pawn Hunter was to sit without a word being spoken.

The Great Pawn Hunter took his place next to another student who was very sad and troubled. The students name was 'The Bad Bishop'. He was always seen planting flowers and weeding the garden outside the detention hall. The Bad Bishop just sat there writing a poem to himself. The poem read:

My lot in life
is weeding plants,
getting in trouble,
stepping on ants.
But some day
I won't be
planting daisies,
in detention,
with all these crazies.
I'll be free
sailing the sea,
without some schemer

> harassing me.
> If you come
> upon my ship,
> don't be brash,
> don't be flip.
> Because this pirate
> shoots from the hip!
> Your mast will fall.
> Your ship will tip
> and you won't give me
> no more lip.
> Yes, I'll be free
> sailing the sea
> without some schemer
> harassing me.

Now, Sarge got up and went out of the room to do an errand. The Great Pawn Hunter asked The Bad Bishop what he was in for. The Bad Bishop told him he was innocent. Some schemer had opened a book inside his desk during a test. Well, The Great Pawn Hunter was surprised to say the least. The Great Pawn Hunter told him his story and they smiled, birds of a feather. Whoever the culprit was, he was a scoundrel.

Now, there was a chess set in the back of the detention room. The Great Pawn Hunter asked about it. The Bad Bishop said that Sarge played the game but he dared not ask him to play. The Bad Bishop was too scared of Sarge. In fact, with all the schemes he had fallen into, he was scared of everyone.

Well, when Sarge came back into the room, The Great Pawn Hunter sat there for a few minutes, trying to build some courage. Then, his hand slowly rose from his desk. "What is it that you want?" said Sarge. The Great Pawn Hunter summoned all the courage he could muster. However, he could only get half his words out. "Could I teach" said The Great Pawn Hunter. Sarge interrupted, "Are you being flip young man?" Sarge got up from his desk and slowly walked over with ruler in hand. Well, The Great Pawn Hunter closed his eyes. This couldn't be happening. Then, he realized he better finish his sentence before he met his agonizing fate. "Could I teach chess to The Bad Bishop?" blurted The Great Pawn Hunter.

Well, Sarge's stern look turned into a smile. "Oh, that's what you were asking," said he. Sarge gave it some thought "Chess does stimulate minds." However, before he could answer, The Great Pawn Hunter said, "I promise I won't get into any more trouble if I can help it." Well, this is all that Sarge needed to hear. He was tough when it came to setting one straight but a marshmallow when one decided to follow the right path. To him, chess was a step in the right direction. Sarge said, "Yes." and pointed them to the chessboard. After The Bad Bishop learned some hypermodern ideas it was clear to The Great Pawn Hunter that The Bad Bishop was a natural, hypermodern player. They played the following hypermodern game of chess, with bishops fianchettoed on the long diagonals. The Bad Bishop played white and The Great Pawn Hunter played black:

The Great Pawn Hunter - 185

1.d4 f5 Dutch Defense

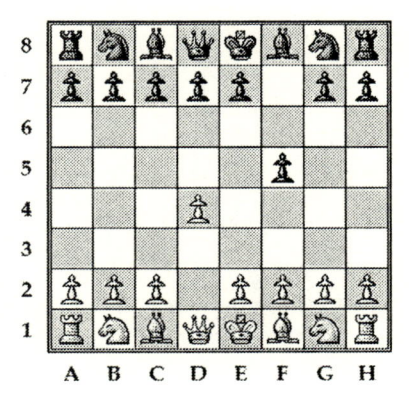

2.g3 Nf6 3.Bg2 g6 Leningrad variation

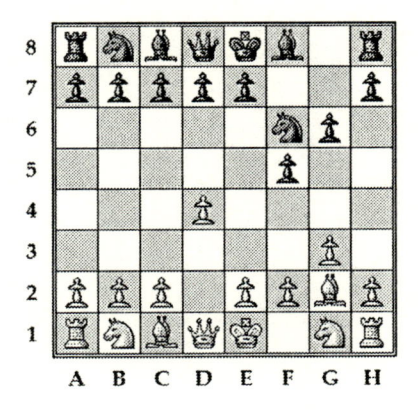

4.b3 Bg7 5.Bb2 d6 6.Nf3 0-0 7.0-0 Ne4 8.Nbd2 Nxd2 9.Qxd2 Nc6 10.Ne1 Qe8

The Great Pawn Hunter - 186

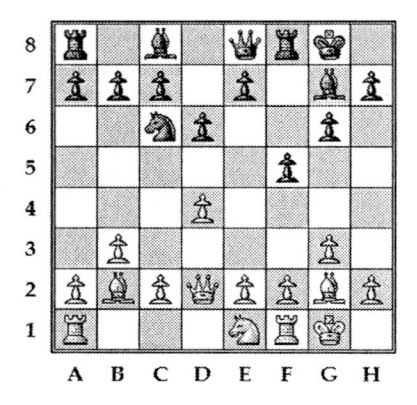

The Great Pawn Hunter gets ready to push his black e pawn to fight for the center.

11.f4 e5 12.Bd5+ Kh8 13.dxe5 dxe5 14.Nd3 exf4

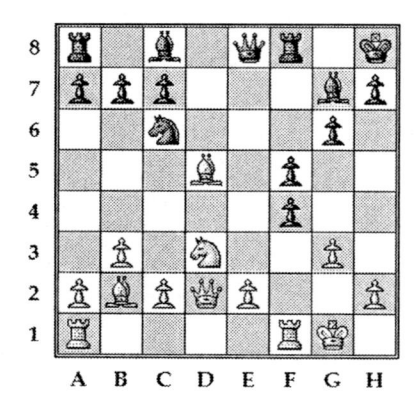

The Bad Bishop is given a backward pawn on the e file. However, The Great Pawn Hunter will find the a1-h8 diagonal is very hard to defend if the black bishop is removed

15.Bxg7+ Kxg7 16.Qxf4 Qe7 17.e4

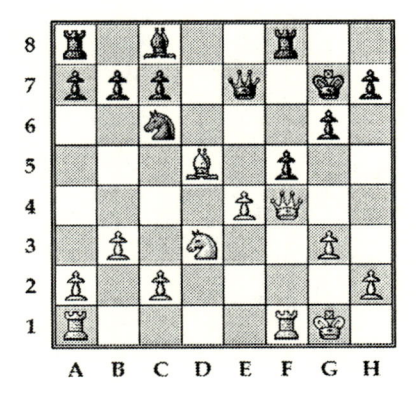

This uses the backward pawn as a battering ram.

17...Nd8 18.exf5 Rxf5 19.Rae1 Be6 20.Qe4 Rxf1+ 21.Rxf1 c6 22.Bxe6 Qxe6

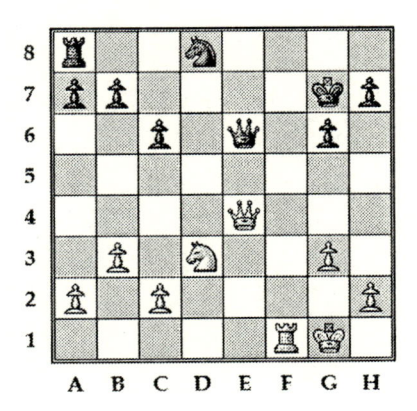

Now The Bad Bishop invades on the a1-h8 diagonal with the white queen.

23.Qd4+ Kg8

The Great Pawn Hunter - 188

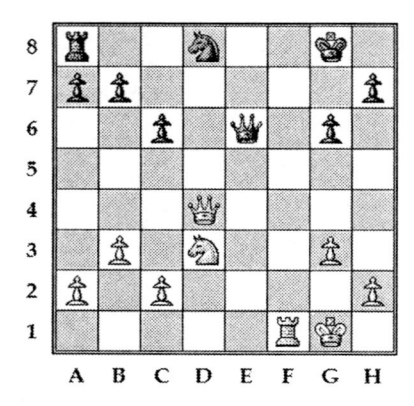

With four attacking white knight moves, it is all over.

24.Ne5 Qe7 25.Ng4 h6 26.Nf6+ Kh8 27.Nd5+

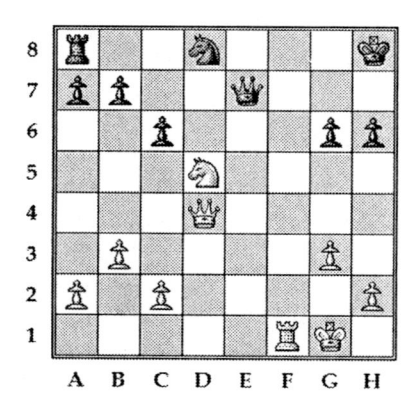

A discovered check, by The Bad Bishop's queen on d4, and The Great Pawn Hunter's black queen falls. The game is over. [27.Nd5+ Qg7 28.Rf8+ Kh7 29.Nf6+] 1-0

After the game was over, they sat back in their seats, Sarge said they could stay inside but he did need two volunteers to work outside in the yard. Well, anything was better than being cooped up in detention hall on a fresh Spring day. The chess players took him up on his offer.

The Bad Bishop weeded the garden. The Great Pawn Hunter started to scrape the rusty old gate of detention hall when Big Louie came up in back of The Great Pawn Hunter. "I have to tell you something." said Big Louie. "I made a terrible mistake." Yes, my friends, she apologized for she came to the sudden realization that it was a surprise test and The Great Pawn Hunter would never had known what page to turn to in the mathematics book. Someone had framed him! Who that someone was, well, you can guess, but I won't tell you.

Now, Big Louie went into the detention hall to talk to Sarge and the prisoners were freed. All they had to do was put their yard tools away. As they closed the rusty old gate to detention hall, The Great Pawn Hunter turned to The Bad Bishop and said "Bad Bishop, there is nothing like your first tournament win. Chess grows on you." "Like a weed?" said The Bad Bishop. "No," said The Great Pawn Hunter, "Like a flower!"

Game
Stohl,I (2550) - Kindermann,S (2565) [A81]
Mitropa Cup Portoroz (3), 1998

Fertile Soil
A poem

A seed needs fertile soil.
It grows for a gardener
who will work and toil.
It's good for the water
to get down to the roots.
Soon, the plant is
covered in shoots.
In Winter months, it's
covered in snow
It waits till Spring
for it to grow.
For everything has a season
and the blossom explains
God's good reason:
To grow, my friends, to grow.

The Great Pawn Hunter

The Igloo Has Landed

The neighborhood was a commotion of events. A snowstorm was raging. The dog was barking wildly. But, there was calmness to this otherwise chaotic scene. For through the howling myriad of snowflakes appeared an old man. He went about his daily routine collecting bottles as if it were a summer's day. Today, Old Maestro had a special errand to do. On him, you could depend...Winter, Spring, Summer, Fall...

Outside The Great Pawn Hunter's house at Eight Mission Avenue, three chess player's gathered for a common goal...igloo building. Now, The Great Pawn Hunter had a shovel shaped like a plow. It was his job to gather the snow into a heap. A small figure patted down the snow pile on all sides. It was The Restless Knight's job to make sure the snow pile was firm and uniform. Once the snow was piled high enough and patted down, it was The Bad Bishop's job to dig out the entrance to "Eight and One Half" Mission Avenue, their new igloo.

Well, they labored well into the afternoon. They stopped only for a cup of hot chocolate from their thermoses to warm their hands and stomachs. But, they dared not go back into their houses. Their snow covered-clothes would melt and they would be drenched to the skin. That would be the end of the igloo building.

Soon, the igloo started to take shape. The Bad Bishop started to dig an entrance tunnel from the west side of the snow pile. He dug so far in that all you could see were the heels of his feet. For, he was belly down on the ground. "Are you done yet?" shouted The Restless Knight into the tunnel. The Bad Bishop replied in a hollowed out voice, "I need more space!" "What did he say?" asked The Great Pawn Hunter to The Restless Knight. Restless replied "I think he said I need more space". Well the walls of the tunnel were already thin as could be, but The Bad Bishop dug away at them. Space he wanted and so he dug and dug and dug. As The Bad Bishop dug out the entrance to the igloo, The Great Pawn Hunter shoveled the discarded snow onto the top of the main snow pile.

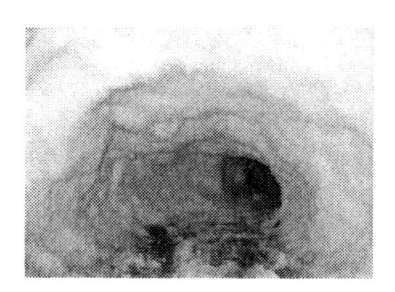

Well, The Bad Bishop had tunneled 5 feet in. He turned onto his back and looked up at the ceiling of the tunnel. Then, tragedy struck! First, a drop of snow fell from the ceiling and landed on his chest. The Bad Bishop said to himself, "This can't be good." Then, Kaboom! The whole tunnel caved in on him. The Great Pawn Hunter and The Restless Knight dug frantically when, out from the middle of the tunnel sprang The Bad Bishop. He stood up with hands in the air and fell back into the snow...a narrow escape. "What were you saying in there?" asked The Restless Knight and The Great Pawn Hunter. The

Bad Bishop replied "Never mind." Then The Bad Bishop stood up, shook the snow off of himself, and looked down at the wrecked tunnel. He was depressed.
However, The Restless Knight was not going to give up. She took a step back and analyzed the situation. "You know," said The Restless Knight "if we wait some hours the snow will harden by itself and we can dig a much better and stronger igloo." The Great Pawn Hunter turned to The Bad Bishop and said "I think she's got a plan." The Bad Bishop with a vote of confidence stated, "Draw up the blueprint Restless. Draw up the blueprint!"

Well, they went to their favorite hang out Castle French Fry. In between munching their French fries and glugging down their sodas, The Great Pawn Hunter added to The Restless Knight's brilliant plan. His idea was to spray the top of the snow pile with water and let it freeze overnight. This, he figured, would make the frame of the igloo much stronger. The Restless Knight designed how the igloo would look inside from the height of the ceiling to the subtle touch of snow shelves that would be built out of the igloo's walls. Now, my friends, see what you can do when you take the time to plan.

They arrived back at "Eight and One Half" Mission Avenue with a plan in hand. They sprayed the snow pile with the water and let mother nature do her thing. The next day they met early. It was still snowing. What a storm! They couldn't tell if it had frozen or not because light snow had built up on top of the snow pile. They just had to rely on the fact that it was below freezing on the thermometer. They started to dig.

The Bad Bishop disappeared into the tunnel...shoulders, waist, and then the feet. Soon, you couldn't see him at all. He turned onto his back and looked up at the ceiling of the tunnel. The sides were frozen. He exclaimed "Yes!" and he dug according to the blueprint that The Restless Knight created.

They had just finished the igloo according to plan. They were all gathered inside when The Bad Bishop noticed legs and a carriage outside the entrance to the igloo. "Who's there?" asked The Bad Bishop to the mysterious pair of legs. The stranger's knees bent and a waistline appeared, then the shoulders, and then a face. It was Old Maestro with some discarded milk crates for the chess players to sit on. They invited him in and offered him a cup of hot chocolate. To show his appreciation, he said he would give them a chess lesson. The Great Pawn Hunter retrieved a pocket chess set from his shirt pocket and Old Maestro went over the following game:

The Great Pawn Hunter - 195

1.e4 Nf6 Alekhine's Defense

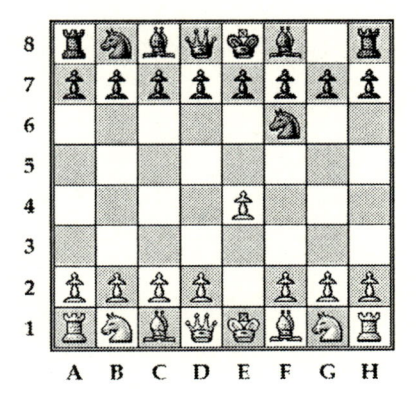

2.e5 Nd5 3.d4 d6 4.c4 Nb6 5.f4 Four Pawn's Attack

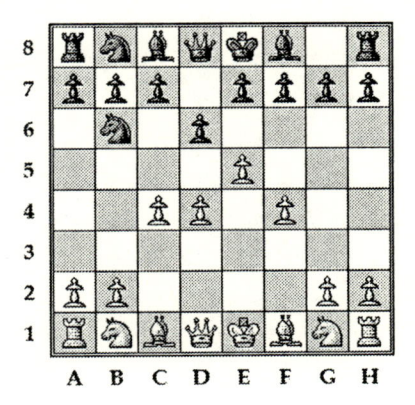

5...f6 6.Bd3 g6 7.f5

The Great Pawn Hunter - 196

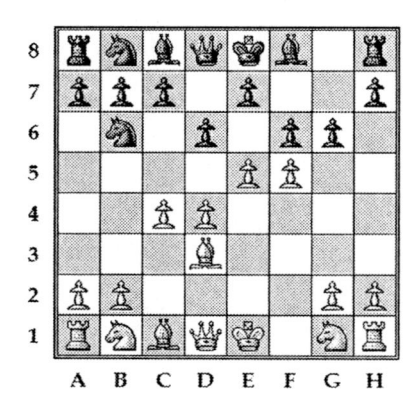

The White Pawn center is far advanced with no troops to support it. It dissolves.

7...dxe5 8.fxg6 Qxd4 9.Nf3 Qg4 10.Qe2 Nc6 11.0-0 Be6 12.Nc3 0-0-0 13.Be3 Nb4 14.Nd5

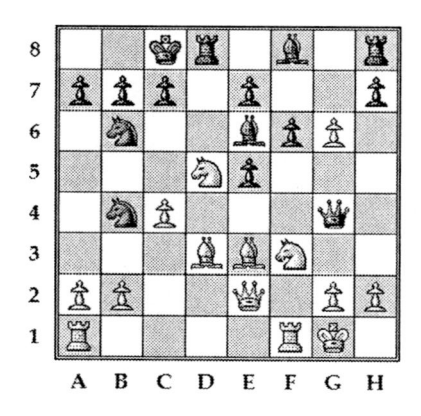

Black lures the White Queen onto the (d) file by trading the knight. There the Queen can be easily attacked by Black's troops.

14...Nxd3 15.Qxd3 e4 16.Nxb6+ axb6 17.Qa3 c5

The Great Pawn Hunter - 197

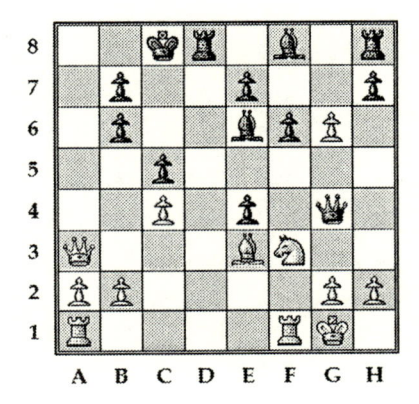

Black builds an escape square for the King on c7 by the pawn push.

18.h3 Qh5 19.Nh2 hxg6 20.Qa8+ Kc7 21.Bf4+ Rd6 22.Bxd6+ exd6 23.Qa3

Hurrying back onto the defense.

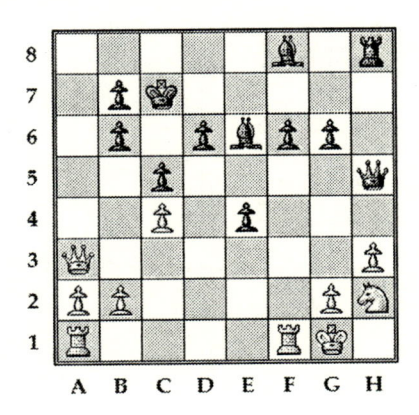

23...Bg7 24.Qg3 f5 25.Rfd1 Be5 26.Qe1 g5

The Great Pawn Hunter - 198

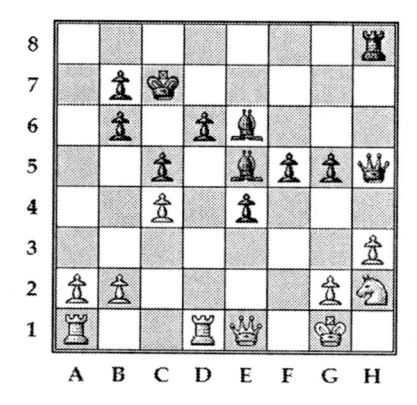

Black uses his (g) pawn to break open the pawn shield surrounding the White King.

27.Nf1 g4 28.h4 g3 29.Nxg3 Qxh4 30.Nf1 Qh1+ 31.Kf2 Bd4+ 32.Rxd4 cxd4

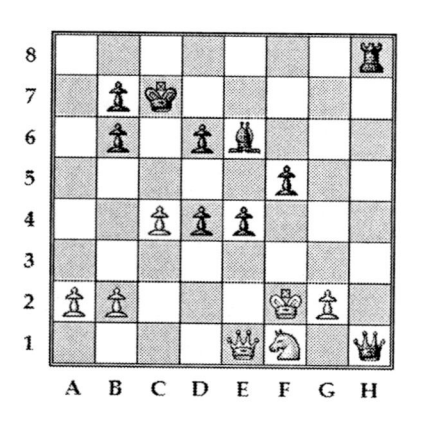

33.b3 e3+ 34.Ke2 Qxg2+

The Great Pawn Hunter - 199

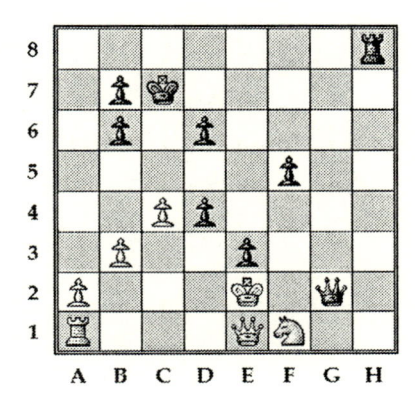

Now it is Black that controls the center with pawns. But this time, the pawns cannot be dissolved by White.

[34...Qxg2+ 35.Kd1 Rh1! ; 34...Qxg2+ 35.Kd3 f4 36.Ng3 fxg3 37.Kxd4 Qb2+ 38.Kd3 Re8 39.Kxe3 Bh3+ 40.Kf3 Qf6+ 41.Kxg3 Qg5+ 42.Kf3 Qg2+ 43.Kf4 Qg4#] 0-1

After the game was over, Old Maestro asked the chess players who would be the next world champion. The Great Pawn Hunter confidently said, "You're looking at him!" The others smiled, reached over, and messed up his hair. My friends, may all your igloos be frosty and may all your friendships be warm.

Game
Papadopoulos,G - Ioannidis,E [B03]
Ambelokipi op 34th Ambelokipi (5), 26.01.2002

The Monkey and the Bee
A poem

"Knowledge is key"
said the monkey
to the bee.
"I eat my bananas
safe high in the tree."
Now, bee to the monkey
said "I'll think about it.
That monkey's no monkey.
He's mentally fit."
So, here is the lesson
from me to learn:
"Sharpen your gippy to
avoid a bad turn."
Just like the monkey
safe high in the tree,
who eats his bananas
and talks to the bees,
That monkey's no monkey
he's mentally fit
"Knowledge is key"
and that's that,
and that's it.

The Great Pawn Hunter

Bits and Bytes

It was a new year at The Great Pawn Hunter's school. Some of the students were to be selected for a special class for learning computers. Alas, The Bad Bishop didn't have the grades like his other friends did. Even The Talker had made the chosen list for he was a naturally gifted scoundrel. It was a shame he used most of his talents for deeds that were, how shall I put it, "Against the grain."...

Well, The Great Pawn Hunter and The Restless Knight went off to their computer class, along with our villain, where they learned how to use the computer for mathematics. This was not The Bad Bishop's strength and that was why he wasn't chosen. When the bell rang to end school for the day, The Great Pawn Hunter and The Restless Knight found The Bad Bishop at Castle French Fry playing chess with Old Maestro. The Bad Bishop was depressed at first, but Old Maestro worked his magic and brought The Bad Bishop out of the dumps. You see, they were playing for fries. A rook was worth five fries, a Knight was worth three fries, a Bishop was worth three fries, a Queen was worth nine fries, and a pawn was worth 1 fry. Now as The Bad Bishop was winning game after game with quick checkmates, Old Maestro was capturing pawns and pieces and taking all the fries. The Bad Bishop didn't know it, but, Old Maestro had checkmate worked out in his mind many times. However, he wanted The Bad Bishop to taste victory and Old Maestro wanted to taste the fries for he was very hungry...the poor old soul. Now The Bad Bishop felt like a million dollars. He must have won five or six games in a row. "Old

Maestro," said The Bad Bishop, "I don't understand. You are a much better player than me. Are you trying to make me feel better by losing?" Old Maestro turned red in the face. His good deed was shown in the light. "Who me?" said Old Maestro, "I tell you what. I'll play you for a root beer".

Now, later on in the day, The Great Pawn Hunter and The Restless Knight joined the group. "How was computer class?" asked The Bad Bishop. "Well," said The Great Pawn Hunter "Sarge is teaching and it feels like detention." The Bad Bishop smiled, "Been there, done that." said he. "I wish we could do something else with computers," said The Restless Knight. Now, by this time Old Maestro was sipping his root beer and making another move on the chessboard. He saw what the others were doing for The Bad Bishop. Old Maestro remarked, "You chess players are natural for computers, you too Bad Bishop." "But why," said The Bad Bishop "I'm terrible at math. To me, one and one is eleven!" Old Maestro smiled and said "Computers are run by logic and you are naturally gifted with this." "What do you mean?" asked The Bad Bishop. Old Maestro asked The Bad Bishop a question "When you play chess, and you are about to make a move, what are your thoughts?" The Bad Bishop replied, "Well, I say to myself 'If I do this then my opponent will do that'." "Ahh," said Old Maestro "That basic 'if/then' statement is at the heart of all computers. It is the logic that drives them. The Bad Bishop replied, "Do you mean to say that I can put my thoughts into the computer and make it think?" "Yes," said Old Maestro "You don't have to be a mathematician. Even The Talker can teach a computer how to think." "Now there's a scary thought." said The Great Pawn

The Great Pawn Hunter - 203

Hunter. "The computer," said Old Maestro, "is just like a new born baby. It knows only what you teach it."

Now, Old Maestro finished making his move on the chessboard. But, this time Old Maestro had to play honestly. He sacrificed a piece and forced the win. "Wow," said The Bad Bishop "You're good." "You played great chess today" said Old Maestro. "Thanks," said The Bad Bishop "How's your soda?" Old Maestro smiled and said "Next time we'll play for chicken nuggets." The following game is Old Maestro's forced win. Old Maestro played the white pieces and The Bad Bishop played the black pieces:

1.d4 Nf6 2.c4 e6 3.Nf3 b6 Queen's Indian Defense **4.g3** Main Line

4...Ba6 5.b3 Bb4+ 6.Bd2 Be7 7.Bg2 c6 8.0-0 d5 9.Qc2 0-0 10.Rd1 Nbd7 11.Bf4 Rc8

The Great Pawn Hunter - 204

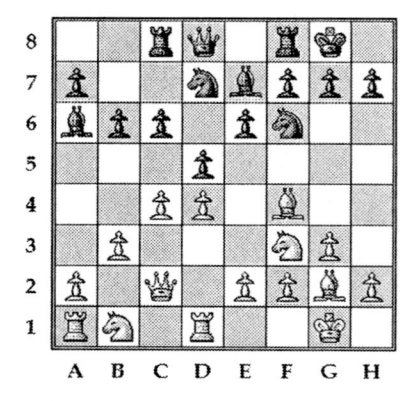

Both rooks have posted themselves on files against the opposing queens. If only they could open the rook's files.

12.Nc3 Nh5 13.Bc1 Nhf6 14.Bb2 dxc4

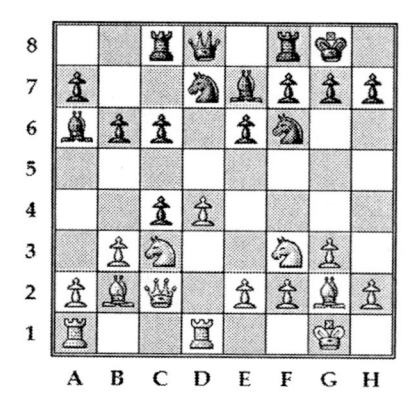

The Bad Bishop decides to win a white pawn.

15.bxc4 Bxc4 16.Ne5 Nxe5 17.dxe5 Nd5 18.Ne4

The Great Pawn Hunter - 205

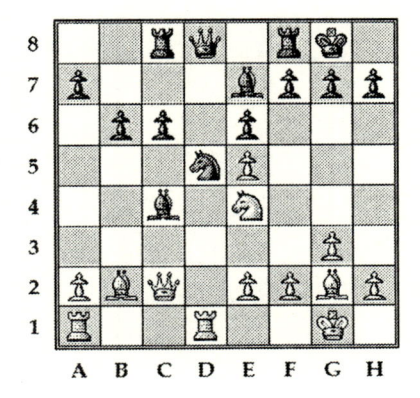

Bringing the knight to e4 behind the e5 pawn is a common plan to occupy the pawn's outposts either on d6 or f6.

18...b5 19.Nd6 Bxd6 20.exd6 Qd7

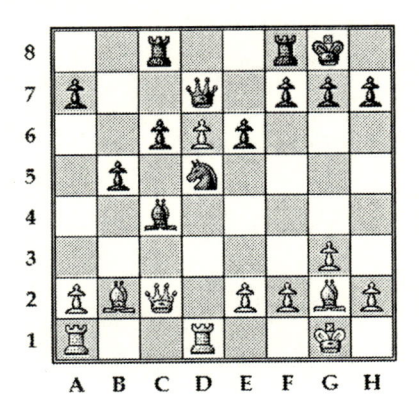

The queen cannot take the pawn because of e4 winning the knight, since the knight would be pinned to the queen. [20...Qxd6 21.e4 Nb4 22.Qc3!]

21.Rd4 f5 22.e4 Nb4 23.Qc3 c5 24.Rd2

The Great Pawn Hunter - 206

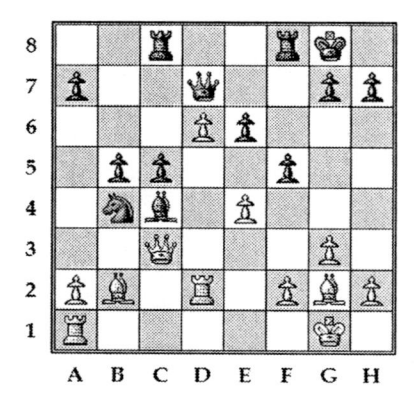

Old Maestro's white queen and bishop attack down the a1-h8 diagonal. If only there was a way to draw The Bad Bishop's queen away from protecting the g7 pawn.

24...f4 25.a4 a6 26.axb5 axb5 27.Ra7

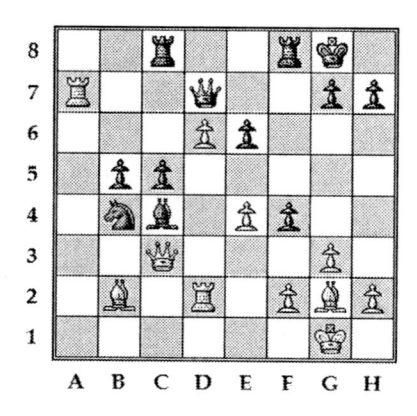

A wonderful sacrifice of the rook. If Qxa7 then d7 breaks the connection of the black queen to the g7 pawn! [27.Ra7 Qxa7 28.d7] 1-0

"Bad Bishop," said The Restless Knight "We have something to tell you. Sarge has made an offer. Any student that can learn how to program a game will earn full credit for his computer class." "Really, but what game can I program." asked The Bad Bishop. Old Maestro said, "How about a simple chess game? You already know the values of the pieces." The Bad Bishop interjected "Now, how many fries was the king?" The chess players laughed. Old Maestro continued, "All you need is a grid of 64 squares. You can put the points of each piece into the squares of the grid. I can teach you how to make the computer know if checkmate is on the board."

Well, Old Maestro spent his days after school teaching The Bad Bishop. They checked and double checked their logic. Everything was ready to give Sarge a demonstration for the following day. The next day came. Sarge and The Bad Bishop sat together. Sarge made his first move on the computer chess game and everything went perfectly. That's when The Talker walked by on his way out of the classroom and said "good luck" to The Bad Bishop. Now, the hairs on the back of The Bad Bishop's neck stood up. The Bad Bishop looked over his shoulder uneasily, until The Talker had left the room. The Bad Bishop went to place a piece for the checkmate and up came the "Blue Screen of Death." It read: "Value error. O is not a number." Sarge said, "I am sorry The Bad Bishop. You only get full credit if the game works." However, Sarge was a good hearted man. "I will tell you what," said Sarge, "I will give you until the end of the semester to work on your program. Good Luck. I will see you then."

The Great Pawn Hunter - 208

The Bad Bishop joined his friends, at Castle French Fry who were eager to learn the outcome of the demonstration. The Bad Bishop told them the news. Old Maestro asked The Bad Bishop, "What was the error message?" The Bad Bishop said "O is not a number, but it is a number. I can't understand why the computer would think so badly." Old Maestro thought a silly thought to himself , "Does it like fries?" The Bad Bishop had tested the program time and time again and this was the fruit of The Bad Bishop's labor...an error message. Well my friends, sometimes things don't go as planned. However, Old Maestro smiled. He had seen this error before. "O is not a number is correct because O is not 0. 0 is zero." This means that somewhere in your program there is a letter 'O' where there should be the number zero.

Well, The Bad Bishop went back to the school and checked. He was looking at his program when on about the thirteenth line down he found the error. He made the correction. How the 'O' got into his program...well, you can guess and your answer is good enough for me. The same day, The Bad Bishop showed his working chess program to Sarge and got full credit for his efforts. It was a testimony to persistence, hard work and good friends. He joined his friends at Castle French Fry with a smile from ear to ear. Together they shared a whole carton of fries and...

Extra Ketchup!!!

Game
Bacrot,E (2653) - Lautier,J (2675) [E15]
Grand Prix du Senat 3rd place Paris (2.1),
30.06.2002

Squirrels' Tails
A poem

Life is blessed
with different things
the squirrels: tails
the angels: wings
Now, if we fight
against our role,
it can hurt our heart.
It can hurt our soul.
We all must measure
what we do best
and leave to God
all the rest.
For every life
affects the whole
and God is pleased
by trying.

The Great Pawn Hunter

The Humming Bird

Sunny days with a little haze. Summer's just a toss from Aprils and Mays and outside the school, The Great Pawn Hunter was playing catch with his friends The Restless Knight and The Bad Bishop. They were waiting for the bell to ring for the start of Math class when Old Maestro came along collecting bottles and humming a tune to his favorite melody. It went:
>Didillee--Di--Dildee--Dildum
>Didillee--Dee--Dildi--Dildum
>Didillee--Li--Dillee--Dilli--Dillee--Dilli--Dillee--Dillum.

"That's a beautiful song you are humming," said the chess players. "Yes," said Old Maestro, "I call it 'The Knight's Waltz." He asked The Restless Knight if she wanted to learn the steps. Restless smiled and said "I'd love to." "Now," Old Maestro said, "take two steps to your right. Then keep your weight on your right foot and drag your left foot to your left one step. When you master this footwork you can move forward or sideways always repeating the same pattern of steps in whatever direction you choose." The chess players clapped as Old Maestro and The Restless Knight danced out the steps to Old Maestro's melody. They finished it off with a full turn and a bow to their endearing audience of two.

Well, the bell sounded for Math class and the chess players had to leave Old Maestro. When the students were gathered in the class, they all took their seats. Now, The Talker walked in minutes after the bell, late as always. He walked by The Great Pawn Hunter's desk on his way to, where else, the back row. The students waited for some time and it became clear that Big Louie, the Math teacher, was not going to show. All the students talked to each other questioning Big Louie's whereabouts. They should have asked The Talker. He knew. For, as The Talker made his way to school, he passed by Big Louie's car which had been broken down with flat tires. It just so happened that one of the tires was marked with a "T"...the mark of, well, you know who. However, my friends, I refuse to believe that The Talker was that diabolical. He was, after all, a chess player like you and me. Even though, some believed, he had no blood in his veins at all.

Well, the Principal, Ms. Harmony, walked in and told the students to quiet down. She said "everyone would have to remain still in their seats for the whole period and she would teach them poetry." The Bad Bishop said to himself, "Just what I need...training for detention." Big Louie's math topic for today, Area, would have to be postponed. Now, The Great Pawn Hunter knew his math well. He knew that "area" was simply measuring the amount of "space" contained in a shape like a square or triangle. He learned about "space" from Old Maestro in a chess lesson who happened to be outside collecting bottles at this very moment. He also knew that Ms. Harmony had a sweet spot for Old Maestro. Well, it didn't take The Great Pawn Hunter very long to put one and one together. He raised his hand and mentioned to Ms. Harmony that Old Maestro could teach them the math subject with chess.
Well Ms. Harmony thought to herself, if Old Maestro didn't mind, it would be a brilliant idea. After all, math is closely related to chess. Ms. Harmony walked out and spoke to Old Maestro. The Great Pawn Hunter,

The Restless Knight and The Bad Bishop looked on from the window. They could see the two figures talking for a few minutes. There was a pause and finally Old Maestro nodded his head in agreement. Ms. Harmony came back into the room with a chess demonstration board and hung it on the chalkboard. Then a hush filled the room as Old Maestro walked in. Ms. Harmony introduced him as a teacher of chess. However, you and I know that Old Maestro is much more than a teacher. A champion from years gone by, Old Maestro was considered to be a chess player's chess player, the highest compliment.

Now, Old Maestro, asked The Restless Knight to come to the front of the room for a demonstration. The Restless Knight walked up to the front of the class, looked at the two adults, and smiled. Then Old Maestro asked if one of the male students would come up to the front of the room to help with the demonstration. Well, The Talker saw this as a perfect opportunity to show off in front of the students. He volunteered. However, when he found out that Old Maestro wanted the two students to dance around in a circle, he thought Old Maestro was surely crazy.

Well, The Restless Knight moved around to her left and The Talker moved to his right and stepped all over her toes. He shouted at The Restless Knight, "You are a lousy dancer. You are supposed to go in the other direction. I don't see how any of this is related to chess!" said he. He thought his trademark thoughts, "plotting and planning is all in a day's work." He smiled a satisfactory smile. Well, Ms. Harmony asked The Talker to take his seat. However, The Talker did have a point.

Ms. Harmony asked Old Maestro, "How does it relate to chess?" Well, this was the very same question that Old Maestro was trying to figure out himself. His mind churned and finally it all gelled like glue...he didn't have a clue. But he was having fun and he didn't let this unsolved problem cloud his mind, which was clouded already. "Principal," he said, "if you just give me a moment to finish my demonstration you will see what I am trying to demonstrate." Whatever that was. This is where Old Maestro implemented his decoy maneuver. He asked Ms. Harmony to take his hands and dance the Knight's Waltz. She thought "I still don't see how it relates." But, she was in front of all those students and she had to give in.

He taught the students his melody and they all whistled it while Old Maestro and Ms. Harmony danced "A Knight's Waltz" down the first aisle and around the room. They came to The Talker's desk and Ms. Harmony put it into high gear, for by now she had the steps memorized. She turned 'The Knight's Waltz' into a Fox Trot and shouted out "Old Maestro, hold on and I'll show you how it's done." They went off down the aisle with loops and turns and finished it off by circling the teacher's desk in the front of the room.

Now, The Talker, shouted out "But, how does it relate to chess?" to put Old Maestro on the spot. However, by this time Old Maestro had the answer. "Old Maestro," questioned The Restless Knight, "what happened when you and The Talker went in the same direction?" Restless replied, "We collided." The students giggled. Then he asked Ms. Harmony, "What happened when you and I danced in a circle during the Knight's Waltz?" Ms. Harmony replied "I moved where I had some space to my left." "Ah," said Old Maestro, "and I moved where I had some space to your right." He went up to the demonstration board and showed the students the following diagram.

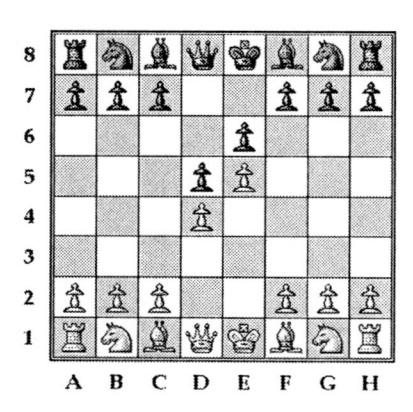

Old Maestro said to Ms. Harmony and the students, "Attack where you have the most space! You see, the white pieces have space on the kingside because the white Pawns on d4 and e5 point to that side of the board. For white, the kingside is the strong side of the board, all because of the pawn structure. The black pieces should attack on the queen side because black's pawns on e6 and d5 point to the queenside. For black, the queenside is the strong side of the board. If you attack where your opponent has most of their pieces, on the weak side of the board, then it is likely that you won't make any headway because you will be stepping on each other's toes. Attacking on the weak side of the board is not in the spirit of your pawn structure. In most situations, only attack on the weak side if you are trying to divert your opponent from your attack on the strong side of the board." Then he showed them the following game:

1.e4 e6 French Defense

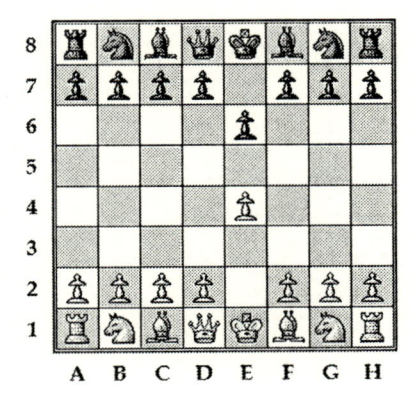

2.d4 d5 3.Nc3 Nf6 4.Bg5 Be7 5.e5 Nfd7 6.Bxe7 Qxe7 Classical Variation

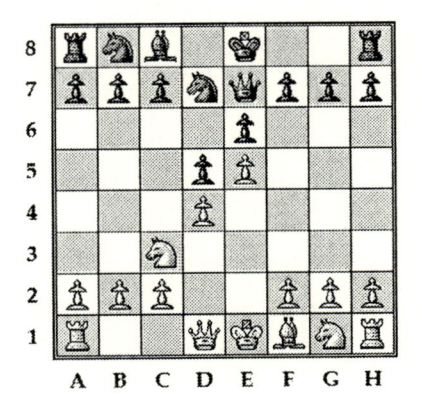

7.f4

The Great Pawn Hunter - 216

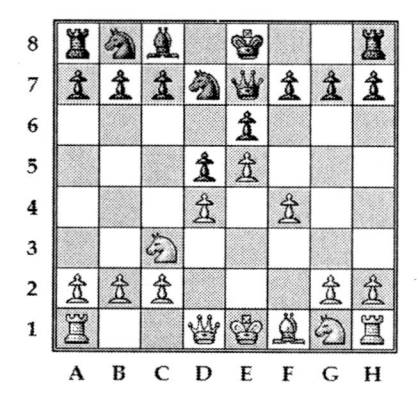

White builds a quartgrip of pawns on (e5,f4,g4,h5). This quartgrip is used to make a "Threat" on the kingside.

7...a6 8.Nf3 c5 9.dxc5 Nc6 10.Bd3 Qxc5 11.Qd2 b5 12.h4 b4 13.Na4 Qa5 14.b3 Nc5 15.Nxc5 Qxc5 16.Rc1

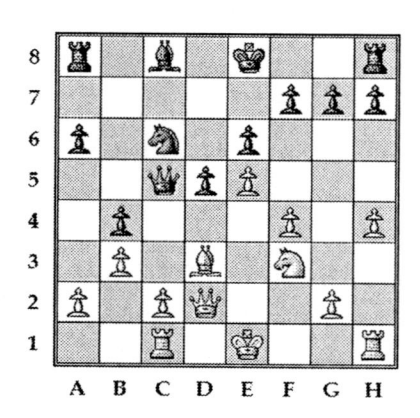

Opposing the queen with a lesser valued piece, like a rook behind a pawn, is a subtle threat.

16...Bd7 17.c4 bxc3 18.Rxc3 Qb6 19.h5 h6 20.Qf2 Qb4 21.Qc5 Qxc5 22.Rxc5 Ke7 23.Kd2 Rhb8 24.Rhc1 Rb6 25.Be2 f6 26.Ke3 Ra7 27.g4

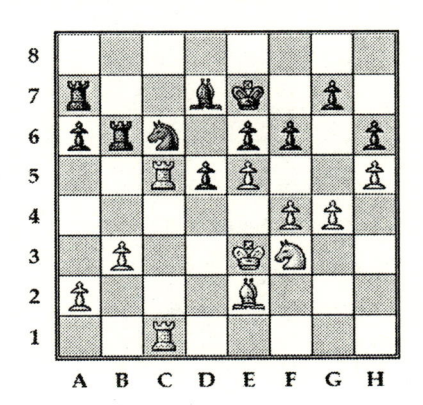

White has made a first "Threat" by attacking on the weak side of the board with rooks. All the opponent's pieces are there. The players are stepping on each other's toes! However, now a second "Threat" is created on the kingside by the Quartgrip. Against advanced players, you need at least two threats to make an attack successful. By alternating threats on two points in Black's camp, White finds the winning plan.

27...a5 28.exf6+ gxf6 29.g5 fxg5 30.fxg5 hxg5

The Great Pawn Hunter - 218

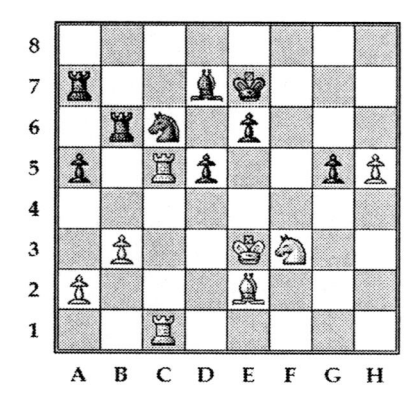

The Quartgrip obtains a pawn majority that produces a Passed Pawn. The Passed Pawn is pushed. This pawn becomes a second "Threat".

31.h6 Ra8 32.Bb5 Kd6 33.h7 d4+ 34.Kd2 e5 35.Nxg5 Rxb5 36.Rxb5 Ke7 37.Rb7

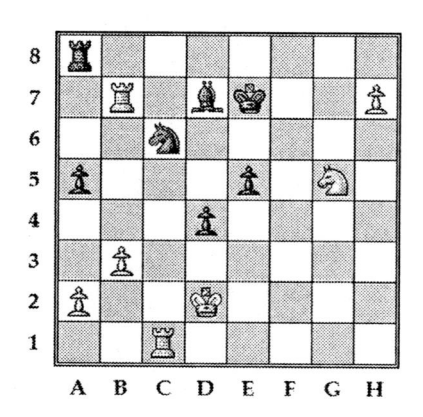

The pin of the bishop wins the day. The c6 knight is threatened. If the knight moves, then white rooks can double on the 7th rank. Or, the rook on b7 can simply sacrifice itself for the bishop. This draws the black king to d7, allowing the knight on g5 to move to the f7 square and the passed pawn on h7 promotes! 1-0

Well, Old Maestro pulled it all together, didn't he. He proved he was quite a great and courageous chess teacher. For, he solved his chess problem, put a scoundrel in his place, and won the heart of Ms. Harmony. All in all, a very eventful day.

Game
Sutovsky(GM) (2652) - C.Hansen(GM) (2610) [C14]
Sigeman Tournament Copenhagen, Denmark (6),
05.05.2003

The Spirit Dove
A poem

A heart's beating
fondest memories
a prayer or two entwined.
Loving adoration
gently brought to mind.
I think of love in silence
my hands against my chest.
A little dove, the spirit of,
upon my heart does rest.
Thumbs: the head
Fingers: the wings
My body sighs.
My spirit sings.
A symbol of endearing love
not of earth but God above.
A faithful watch I'm keeping
this night
this gentle knight.

The Great Pawn Hunter

Coming Home

Summer burst upon the mountains, down the meadows, and into the great city. Crowds could be heard cheering in the baseball park as the boys of summer took the field. Now, The Restless Knight, The Great Pawn Hunter, and The Bad Bishop were in the bleacher section of the stadium enjoying the baseball game. It was the seventh inning stretch and the chess players thought they could squeeze in a 5 minute game of blitz. The Restless Knight pulled her pocket chess set out from her shirt pocket for her friends to play the following game of chess. The Great Pawn Hunter played white and The Bad Bishop played black:

1.d4 Nf6 2.c4 g6 King's Indian Defense

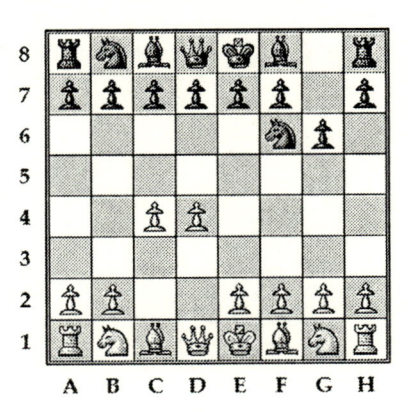

3.Nc3 Bg7 4.e4 d6 5.f3 Samisch Variation

The Great Pawn Hunter - 222

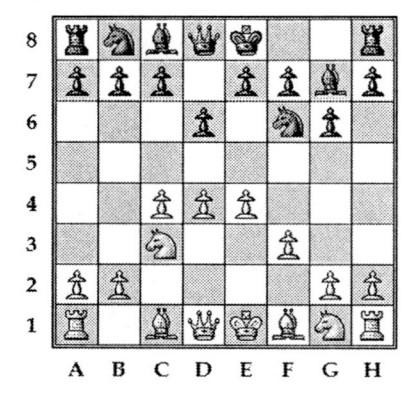

The move f3 supports e4 and keeps an enemy bishop or knight from occupying g4.

5...0-0 6.Bg5 c5

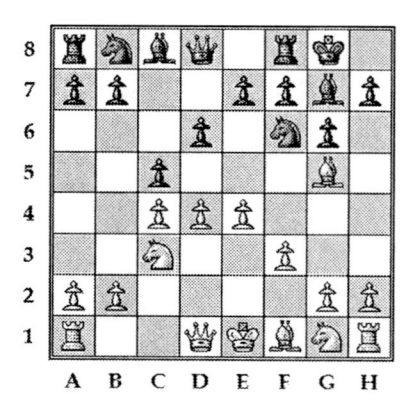

The Bad Bishop attacks the white center d4 pawn with the c5 pawn lever coercing it to advance.

7.d5 h6 8.Be3 e6

The Great Pawn Hunter - 223

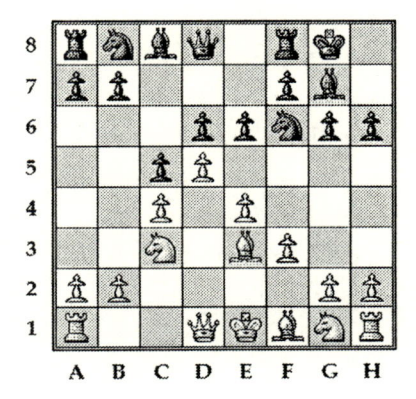

The Bad Bishop's pawn lever e6 challenges the center again.

9.Qd2 exd5 10.cxd5 Re8 11.Be2 h5 12.Bd1 a6 13.a4 Nbd7 14.Nge2 Ne5 15.b3 Bd7 16.0-0 b5

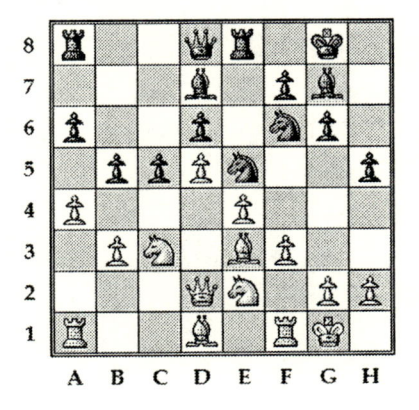

and here comes the queen side attack

The Great Pawn Hunter - 224

**17.Bc2 b4 18.Nd1 a5 19.Nf2 Bc8 20.h3 Ba6
21.Rfe1 Rc8 22.Rac1 Bxe2N 23.Qxe2 c4 24.f4 Nd3
25.Bxd3 cxd3 26.Qxd3 Rxc1 27.Rxc1 Nxe4
28.Nxe4 Qe7 29.Bb6 Qxe4 30.Qxe4 Rxe4**

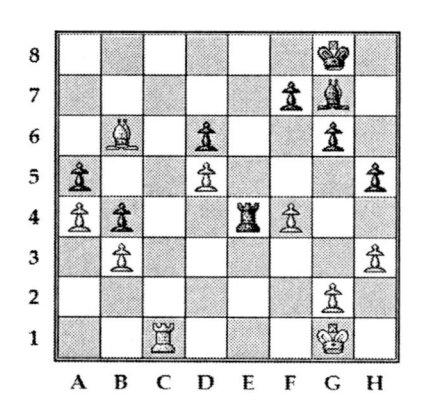

Now, The Great Pawn Hunter playing white snatches a pawn. However, my friends, the pawn is poisoned as you will see.

**31.Bxa5 Bd4+ 32.Kh1 Bc5 33.Bc7 Rd4 34.a5 Rxd5
35.Bb8 Rd2 36.Ra1**

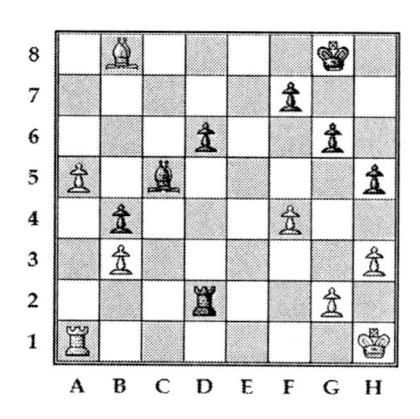

The Great Pawn Hunter - 225

The Great Pawn Hunter is allured by queening his pawn. But, danger is lurking on the horizon!

36...Bd4 37.Ra4 h4 38.a6 Rd1+ 39.Kh2 Bg1+ 40.Kh1 Bf2+ [40...Bf2+ 41.Kh2 Bg3#] 0-1

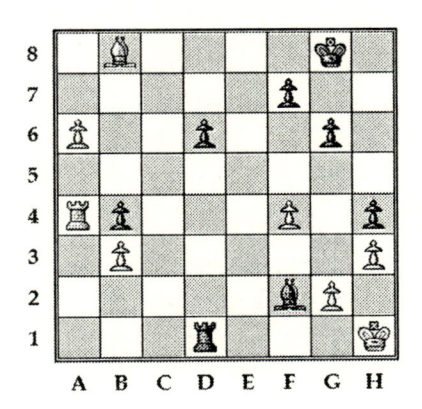

Now, after the chess game was over, the chess players were waiting for their favorite hitter, the Slugger, who was waiting on deck to come up to the plate. There were two outs and two men on base. The pitch count was full, three balls and two strikes. The pitcher delivered his final pitch low and outside for ball four. My friends, the pitcher walked him. The Great Pawn Hunter mentioned to his friends "It's just another walk in the park." The Bad Bishop replied, "The Slugger is up next and the bases are loaded." The Restless Knight added, "He's been struggling the whole game. I hope he hits one out of here."

Well, there was a good reason for his struggling, my friends, for he struggled his whole life and right about now he was doing a little bit of soul searching. The Slugger stepped into the batter's box. Boo's came from all over the stadium. He was in the biggest slump of his career. He thought to himself of long ago in his boyhood days. The Slugger remembered the time he gave his glove to a friend and went up to bat. The friend was not the most attentive and the glove disappeared without a trace. Well, the Slugger looked over towards the dugout uneasily. He could see his glove where he left it. He muttered to himself, "Where's the love?"

The pitcher drilled a fast ball. The Slugger took a mad swing. The pitch was in there for a called strike one. The opposing fans in the stands could be heard shouting, "No Batter, No Batter, No Batter!" The Slugger got ready for another pitch. He thought back to his young adult years. He remembered how he was pulled into an alley and beaten up. Those were tough times. The pitcher went into his set stance ready to deliver another pitch. The Slugger muttered to himself again, "Where's the love?" He swung even more violently but the pitch was a cutter inside and he missed completely. The Umpire called "Strike Two!" He was down to his last strike.

Now, friends, when someone is down and blue there should be someone there to pick them up. However, the uplifting remarks from the bleachers couldn't be heard from the batter's box. The pitcher went into his set stance again. The Slugger thought back to a day before when he walked passed a few chess players playing the game next to a beautiful white building. The Slugger stopped and gazed at the white building and at its steeple rising high into the sky. An old man came by collecting bottles. The Slugger noticed the bond between the chess players and the old man. He thought to himself, "There...there's the love." He firmly placed his feet. The pitcher delivered...and the Slugger swung!

The ball was hit long and deep. The announcer shouted into his microphone, "It's a high fly ball to deep right center. Way back. Way back. It's gone over the bleachers, a Home Run!!!" Now, the chess players saw the ball fly right over their heads and out of the park and The Great Pawn Hunter said to himself, as the Slugger rounded the last base, "Welcome home Slugger, Welcome home."

Game
Brossard,A (2218) - Hernandez,G (2547) [A65]
FRA-chT2 FRA (6), 01.2002

Inches, Minutes, Miles
A poem

In a world of fear and terror
of which I am cast.
I pray Jesus break my fall love
and raise me on the last.
Now days past, a priest told me
"This struggle you're going through
Well, son don't give up,
it's what God wants of you."
I confess dear friends
my soul is down and blue.
But, my Bible tells me persevere
He'll save you in the end.
Well, is it true? Is it true?
Please be true.
Now, I don't know if
what I say or what I do
falls on fertile soil.
But, the other day, I made a meal
unleavened bread and olive oil.
I left it before my crucifix
for God so meek and mild
and a voice within me bellowed out
"It's acceptable"
My friends, my whole being smiled.
For once I did good
and it reached God in his throne.
And, for once I felt in my whole life
that I was not alone.
And, I realized God of Heaven
is with me when I'm blue.
He's within each one of us
and what we feel, he feels too.

So, I ask you don't give up,
an offering we can send:
our sorrows, trials, fears and smiles.
A share of love for God above.
Along life's road:
inches, minutes, miles
in Whom our hearts
can mend.

The Great Pawn Hunter

The Great Pawn Hunter - 230

Pebbles

Hot humid air hung heavy over the tables of Castle French Fry. The Great Pawn Hunter and The Restless Knight were in the heat of battle playing a chess game. The Great Pawn Hunter played white and The Restless Knight played black:

1.d4 Nf6 2.c4 c5 3.d5 b5 Benko Gambit.

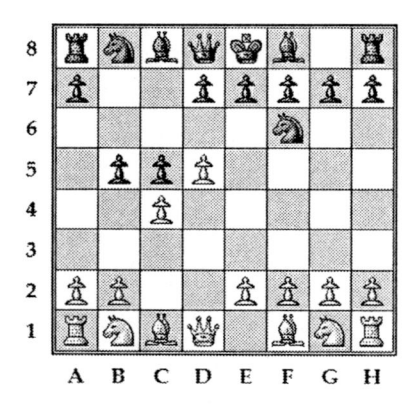

4.cxb5 a6 5.bxa6 e6 6.Nc3 Nxd5 7.Nxd5 exd5 8.Qxd5 Nc6 9.e3 Be7 10.Nf3 0-0 11.Bd2 Qb6 12.Qb3 Qa7 13.Bc3 Bxa6 14.Qa4 Bxf1

The Great Pawn Hunter - 231

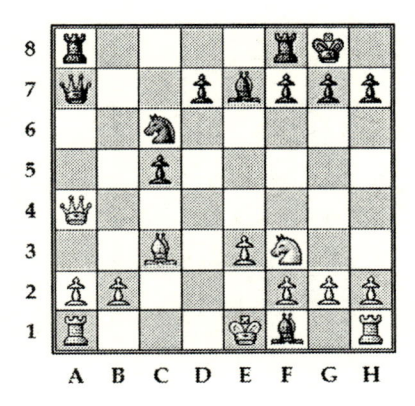

With Bxf1, The Great Pawn Hunter's chance to castle kingside is ruined.

15.Qg4 g6 16.Kxf1 d5 17.h4 h5 18.Qf4 Rad8 19.Rh3 d4 20.exd4 cxd4 21.Bd2 Qb6 22.b3 Nb4

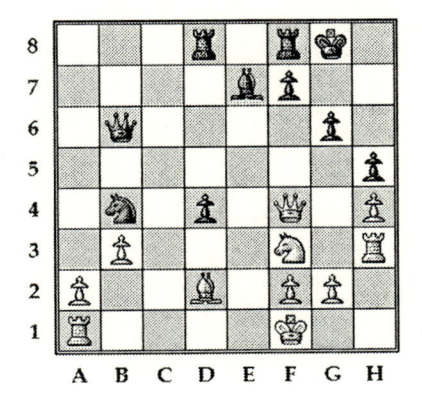

The Restless Knight maneuvers her knight to the center.

23.Rg3 Nd5 24.Qh6 Bf6 25.Ng5 Bxg5 26.Bxg5 Rc8 27.Bd2 Rc2 28.Re1 Qf6 29.Kg1 Rxa2 30.Rf3 Qd6

The Great Pawn Hunter - 232

31.Rd3 Ne7 32.Rf3 Nd5 33.Qg5 Rfa8 34.Rd3 Nb4 35.Bf4 Qxf4!

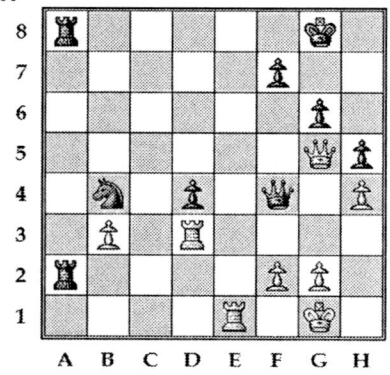

A stunning sacrifice of the queen leaves all of The Great Pawn Hunter's pieces undefended!

36.Qxf4

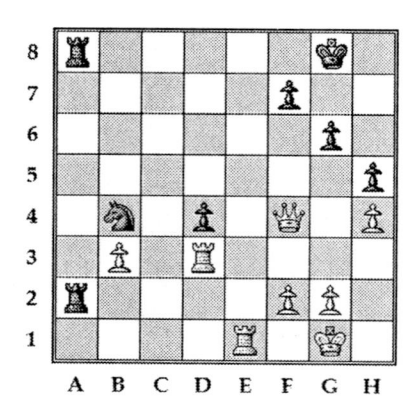

And now The Restless Knight makes nine attacking knight moves...a fitting number.

36...Nxd3 37.Qxd4 Nxe1 38.b4 Nc2 39.Qc3 Na3 40.g4 Nb1 41.Qc5 Nd2 42.gxh5 Nf3+ 43.Kg2 Nxh4+ 44.Kh3 Nf5 45.hxg6 fxg6 46.b5 Kh7 47.b6 R8a3+ 48.Kg4 Ra4+ 49.Kf3 Rc2 50.Qe5 Ra3+ 51.Kg4 Nh6+ 52.Kh4 Rc4+ 53.f4

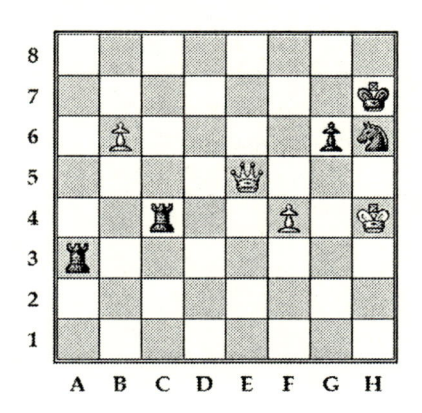

She finishes it off in style ...goodknight.

53...Nf7!

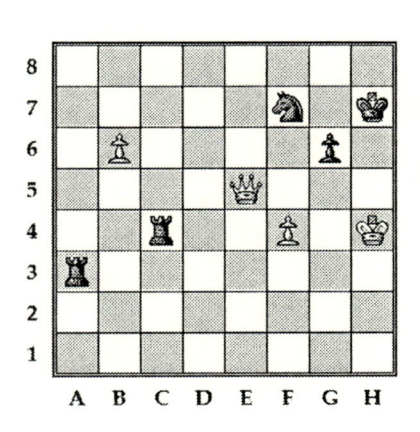

[53...Nf7 54.Qf6 g5+ 55.Kg4 Rxf4+ 56.Qxf4 gxf4 57.Kxf4 Rb3] 0-1

Now, Restless was smiling a successful smile, after her win, when something caught her attention in the front of the building. She lifted her eyes and stared out the window. Through the window, Restless could see a chess player cruising his bicycle to a stop. On the spokes of his bicycle was a playing card, the ace of spades. He dismounted his bicycle. The Restless Knight watched the entrance way. The doors to Castle French Fry burst open and the chess player entered, black boots, black jeans, black t-shirt. My friends, if clothes could say villain, this chess player had them in spades.

The Talker walked over to The Restless Knight and said, "You know what I'm here for Restless. Give me the answer to the Knight's Tour!" The Talker held out his hand and said, "C'mon Restless, hand it over." The Restless Knight reached into her shirt pocket, stretched out her hand, and dropped the answer to the Knight's Tour into The Talker's eager clutches...

How, my friends, could Restless do such a thing as cooperate with a villain? Well, to understand her actions, I must bring you back to the events of the week before when the school had its outing at the bench by the brook. All the students brought their fishing poles, pails and bait. Most were busy trying to land that lunker of a fish except The Great Pawn Hunter, The Restless Knight and The Bad Bishop who were trying to solve the Knight's Tour on a chess set at the picnic bench. The Talker was busy casting from the shore. Well, our chess playing friends had no luck with the chess problem. They tried and tried but to no avail. "I wish Old Maestro was here. He could help us solve the problem," said

The Restless Knight. "Girls can't solve the Knight's Tour," shouted The Talker, "They don't have it in them."

Well, The Restless Knight shouted back "I can so solve the Knight's Tour." The Talker replied, "I'll give you a whole week to solve the problem. If you can't solve it in a week, everyone will know girls can't solve chess problems." The Restless Knight replied back, "I'll have it solved. You can bet on it!" The Talker replied, "Then swear on it." Restless said "Swear on what, I don't have anything to swear on in the first place." The Talker replied, "Then swear on your fishing lure." So, my friends, she did.

Now, The Talker didn't know how to solve the Knight's Tour either. Its secret had always escaped him. This way he would know the answer without even lifting a finger. He had every bit of confidence in The Restless Knight and he was going to use it to his advantage. Yes, my friends, "Plotting and planning is all in a day's work."

It was at this point that The Talker got a bite on his fishing rod. He pulled mightily to set the hook and reeled the fish in. When he pulled it out of the water, it was only a minnow. He launched the fish into the grass behind him. No, my friends, there was not an ounce of compassion in his hollow heart. Restless saw where the minnow landed. She ran over and gently picked it up. However, the poor thing had an injury. So, Restless put the minnow into her pail of water. She took it home and placed it in her fish tank.

The Great Pawn Hunter - 236

Now, every so often, Restless would come over to the tank and spend some time with "Pebbles." She gave this name to the fish because it was always digging up pebbles at the bottom of the tank. It was towards the end of the week that The Restless Knight got desperate. She had no luck, as yet, solving the problem of the Knight's Tour. She didn't notice Pebbles leaping up into the air and splashing back into the water behind her because she was very focused. However, this didn't last long. Pebbles leaped higher and higher and on the third leap he was airborne and sailed out of the tank landing, on the counter top, with a thud. Restless turned around and shouted, "NO! PEBBLES!!!"

She picked up poor Pebbles and placed him back into the tank. However, Pebbles sadly went belly up. My friends, when a fish goes belly up, it is not a good sign. But, God shines His love on all creatures. After a second or two, Pebbles righted himself and swam back down to the bottom of the tank. Now, Restless was relieved to say the least. She peered down through the water and happily watched as Pebbles went back to his pebble digging. It was as he was digging she noticed that his pebbles formed a curious pattern. Restless blinked...then...she blinked again. For the pebbles that Pebbles was digging were curiously arranged by the minnow in patterns that resembled her Knight's Tour. She went back to her chess board and discovered that Pebbles had solved the problem aquatically...and they say fish don't have brains. Well, this one did and it is the honest truth. And, yes, I even swear on my fishing lure!

The Great Pawn Hunter - 237

So, The Talker got what he wanted, the answer to the Knight's Tour ...in a fist full of pebbles, and he remained as confused as he always was for he used his naturally gifted talents for deeds that were...against the grain.

As for the answer to the Knight's Tour, well, I won't keep you waiting:

Knight's Tour

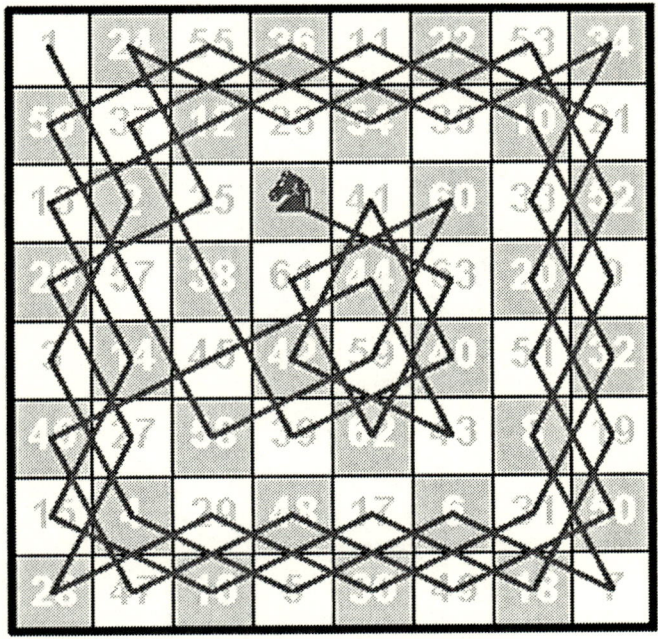

By Dan Thomasson, July 2, 2001
DTHOMASSON@carolina.rr.com

Game
Gunawan,R (2460) - Rogers,I (2475) [A58]
Thessaloniki ol (Men) Thessaloniki (11), 30.11.1984

What's In A Ring
A poem

"What's in a ring?"
said the Queen to the King.
"I sweep the whole board
as you sit on the wing
and what do I get
as you sit in your castle?
I am chased by knights
and bishops and pawns
what a hassle!"
"Dear Queen," said the King
who was so very wise
"To me you're a star.
You belong in the skies
not stuck here with me
on the very first row.
I Don't deserve you,
but I love you so.
If you stay here with me,
I'll make you nine stars
to adorn your crown
like Jupiter and Mars
who sit in the heavens
and reflect the sun's light
on your gentle sweet face
that I dream of at night."
Now, the King narrowly escaped
with his head that day
and if there is a lesson,
I know it would say:
"When your Queen is fighting
with you not your foe,
treat her with kindness

don't step on her toe
and one more thing,
as the clock surely ticks,
pile it higher and deeper
throw it goodn strong
so it sticks!"

The Great Pawn Hunter

The Great Pawn Hunter - 240

The Pursuit of Happiness

The sun was glowing through a crystal blue sky on a clear spring day. The warmth of the sun, cut the morning chill in the park where the derby was being held. The Restless Knight and The Bad Bishop were watching the horses from the fence at the side of the park. They were in awe of the speed and swiftness as the riders galloped by, each testing the others metal...and our chess playing friends were doing the same in a heated game of chess. The Restless Knight played black and The Bad Bishop played White in the following game:

1.d4 Nf6 2.c4 g6 King's Indian Defense

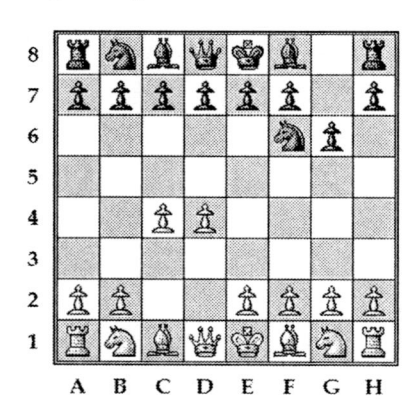

3.Nc3 Bg7 4.e4 0-0 5.Nf3 Classical

The Great Pawn Hunter - 241

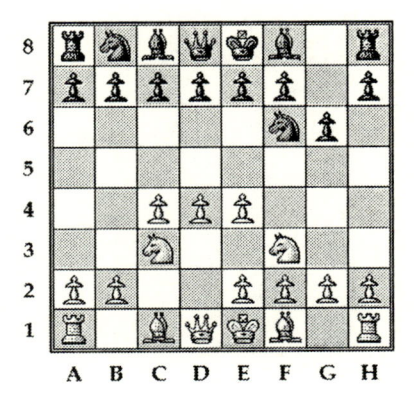

5...c6 6.Be2 d5 7.e5 Ne4 8.0-0 Na6 9.Be3 Nxc3 10.bxc3 Nc7 11.Qd2 Bg4

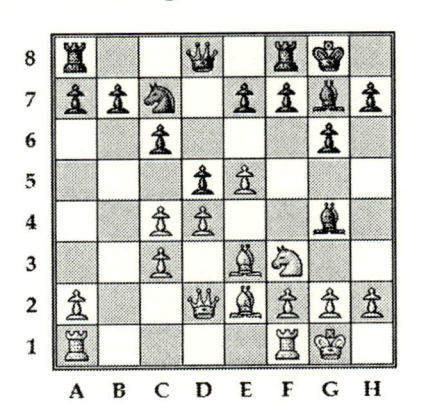

With the center closed, knights are usually more effective than the bishops. So The Restless Knight intends to eliminate The Bad Bishop's knight and keep the center closed for her knight. The Bad Bishop will try to open the center for his bishops.

12.Rab1 Rb8 13.cxd5 Nxd5 14.h3 Bxf3 15.Bxf3 b5

The Great Pawn Hunter - 242

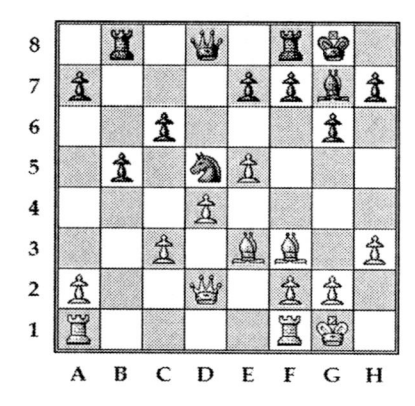

with b5, Restless keeps The Bad Bishop from chasing the knight off of d5 with the move c4. This is key to keeping outposts active. Bxd5 would bring the black queen into the center.

16.Bg5 Qc7 17.Rfe1 a6 18.Rbc1 Nb6 19.e6 Nc4

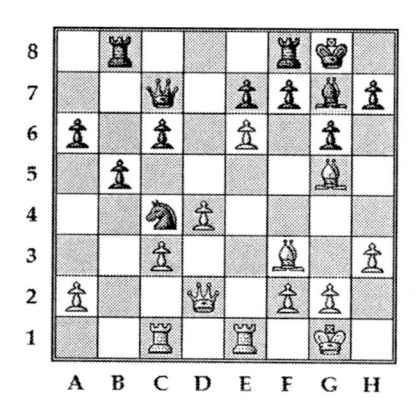

Occupying outposts with the knight keeps the white bishops at bay.

20.Qf4 Nd6 21.Qg3 f5 22.c4

The Great Pawn Hunter - 243

e6 and c4 is all about opening files and diagonals (lines) for The Bad Bishop's pieces

22...bxc4 23.Rxc4

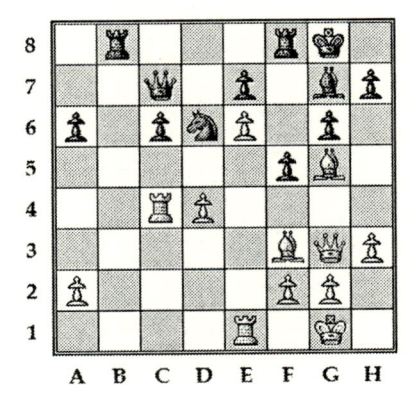

The Bad Bishop thinks he can take advantage of Restless' knight on d6 being pinned to its own queen, since the queen is undefended the knight cannot move. However, The Bad Bishop doesn't realize that the black queen can move instead to create a double attack!

23...Qa5 24.Rcc1 f4 25.Bxf4 Nf5

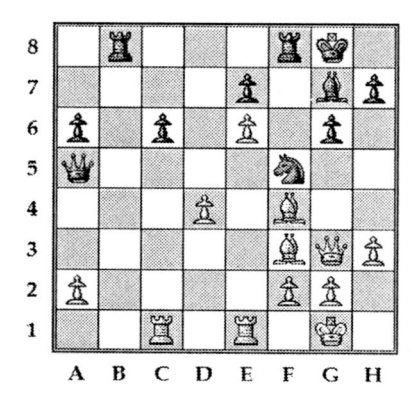

The knight dominates the position.

26.Qg5 Rb2

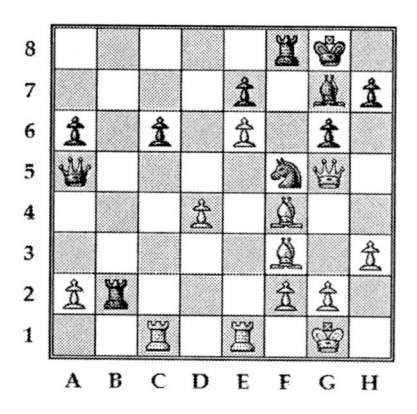

Getting your "rooks on the seventh" is a popular maxim of chess.

27.Re5 Bxe5 28.Bxe5

The Great Pawn Hunter - 245

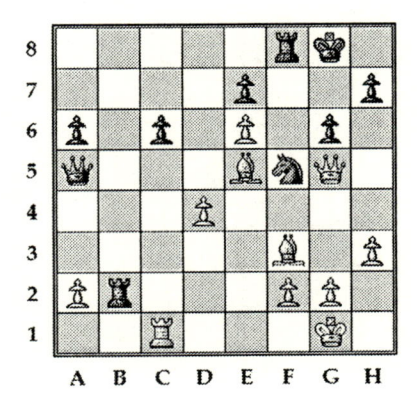

The Bad Bishop's own white queen is unguarded and The Restless Knight uses this to snatch the d pawn.

28...Nxd4 29.Rd1 Rb5 Pin it and win it

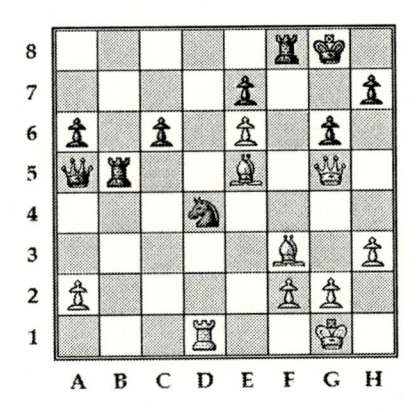

30.Qxe7 Rxe5 31.Rxd4

The Great Pawn Hunter - 246

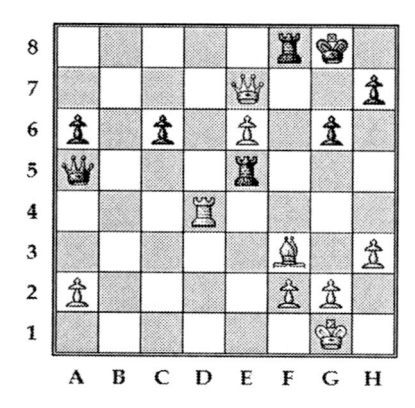

Now The Bad Bishop's rook on d4 is unguarded. Do you see the moves?

31...Re1+ 32.Kh2 Qe5+ 0-1

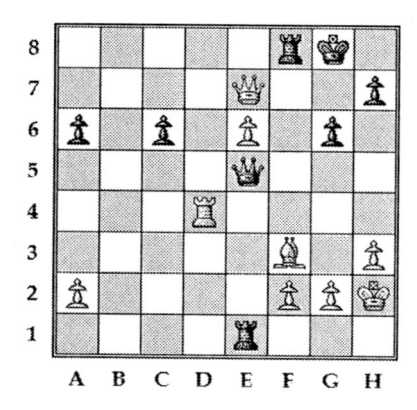

Now after the game was over The Talker approached them from the West. The Talker was always interested in sport...chess that is...just like our friends...at least we can say we all have that in common, God Bless us. As he approached, he could hear The Restless Knight and The Bad Bishop going over the horses' merits. First there was "Lightening." He blew by them in a flash and all they could see was the shine off of his rider's boots. The next horse went by so loudly that all you could hear was the rumble, hence the name..."Thunder". He was fast too, so fast that, well, lets just say he was faster than a millipede running from a vacuum cleaner. Man that's fast. The Talker picked Thunder to win the Derby because he liked the name. However there was an even more formidable horse in the barn, so to speak, and his name was "Happiness". He was, at this moment, approaching them from the East. Now this horse lived a meeker life. With a yoke upon his shoulders, he pulled a cart for his keep. This cart was filled with empty bottles that the driver exchanged for five cents a bottle at the local store. The driver was sitting with his legs dangling over the sides of the cart. The Great Pawn Hunter was holding on for dear life at the other end, desperately trying to keep the bottles from popping off the cart.

The Talker saw the cart approaching. He was in a very good mood. However, you might as well pray for water to boil. For as Old Maestro and The Great Pawn Hunter passed the park, The Talker let out a comment he couldn't help. It just bubbled out of him..."That horse of yours is as good as glue!" said he...a remark perfectly in tune with his mischievous self. Now at that moment, quite by accident, at least we think, a bottle popped off of the back of the cart and beaned The Talker square off of the gippy. The horse and cart trundled past leaving The Talker rubbing his head. Yes, justice was served for the moment. But, it was a terrible waste of a nickel don't you think?

The Great Pawn Hunter - 248

After exchanging the bottles at the store, Old Maestro and The Great Pawn Hunter were on the way back when they heard the bells from the church chiming there melody. Old Maestro raised an eyebrow and looked at The Great Pawn Hunter. The Great Pawn Hunter raised an eyebrow and looked at Old Maestro. For you see, Mass was starting and they were the ones to do the collection. Well, Old Maestro shouted, "Giddy Up" and Happiness sped down the road past the field where the derby was. He caught up to Lightening and Thunder in their heat and galloped passed both in a heartbeat to win by a nose. Now, at the end of the track, Happiness didn't stop at the fence. He road on by. Old Maestro pulled in on the reigns to slow Happiness down but the horse seemed determined to hear Sunday's readings from the pulpit. The chess players chased Happiness up the road and each one got on board the cart with a hand up and a little luck. Yes, even The Talker with a bit of running went to Sunday Mass that day.

Days later, Old Maestro was asked a question by a betting man, "Old Maestro, tell me the secret of Happiness." Now, Old Maestro was very wise. He told him he picked the horse because it had the longest legs. However, the chess players knew the secret of Happiness was in the heart.

Game
Alfred,N (2251) - Bogza,A (2270) [E70]
Budapest FS11 IM Budapest (6), 07.11.2002

An Usher at the Rectory Door
A poem

There's a trip to Tahiti
in this here collection.
Father, what should I do?
I've been waiting out here
at the rectory door
three rings
and still waiting for you.

Are you testing my faith?
How long shall I wait?
This loot weighs heavy
on my soul.
There's a trip to Tahiti
in this here collection.
Come quickly,
before I get rolled.

Now, I don't want to sin.
Father, please let me in.
I don't want to say that you're slow.
But, I've been waiting out here
at the rectory door
since two "holy decades" ago.
And, I pray for some grace
to help me erase
what's roaming the caverns
of my mind:
A pink colored drink
with a little umbrella
...placed just so
to help me unwind.

The Great Pawn Hunter - 250

And, the sun and the sea
is calling to me.
Lord Jesus, give me some peace.
For, as long as I wait,
the temptation is great.
Could I harder pray?
Maybe May?
Surely they'll cease.

Now, as the Rosary was said,
the priest rose from his bed
and answered the call
at his door.
And, the priest asked the usher
"Trip to Tahiti today?"
And the usher just smiled and said:

"Father, there were pink little umbrellas
placed just so."
Well, Father nodded his head
and took the collection.
There were pink little umbrellas
no more.

So, when you have the sun and the sea
calling you to Tahiti
Think of the Usher and sing
the small little beads
called the "Rosary."
She will cure you
of the serpent's sting.

The Great Pawn Hunter

The Great Pawn Hunter - 251

Where Rainbows Arch

A more curious adventure an outing never was than this day's adventure at the park. There were elephants and 'go carts', swimming, and even a skywriting plane for the bold and daring. Now, on their journey there, our chess playing friends found they all had unique interests...all except The Talker who wanted to go 'go carting' with The Restless Knight. He had something to prove...a vendetta as it were. The Bad Bishop wanted to see the elephants. The Great Pawn Hunter wanted to go swimming. The only truly adventurous soul in the group was Old Maestro. He opted for the skywriting tour and was busily engaged in a chess game as we speak. Old Maestro played black and The Great Pawn Hunter played white:

1.e4 c5 Sicilian Defense

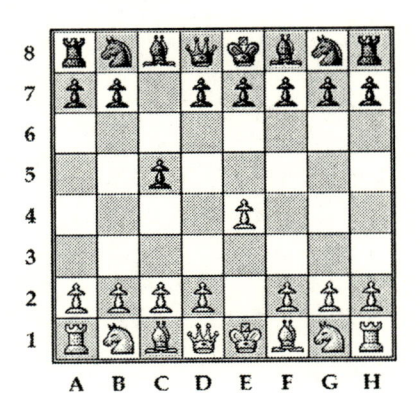

2.Nf3 e6 3.d3 Nc6 4.g3 g6 Closed Variation.

The Great Pawn Hunter - 252

Old Maestro looks to prevent d4 by The Great Pawn Hunter.

5.Bg5 Qc7 6.Bg2 Bg7 7.c3 Nge7 8.0-0 0-0 9.Be3 b6 10.Na3 Ba6 11.Re1 d5 12.exd5 Nxd5

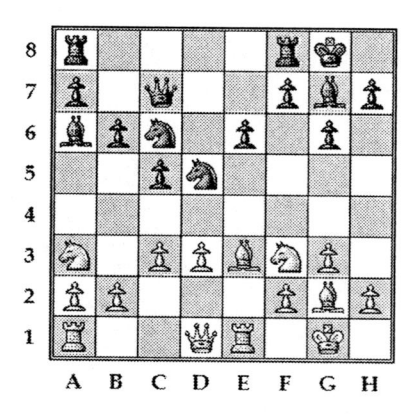

With Nxd5, Old Maestro forces a backward pawn on an open file (d3). Also if the e6 pawn were to take, the pawn structures would be symmetrical which can lead to a draw.

The Great Pawn Hunter - 253

13.Bg5 h6 14.Bc1 Rad8 15.Qc2 Rd7 16.Nc4 Rfd8 17.a4

With (a4), The Great Pawn Hunter looks to strengthen his white c4 knight's outpost by preventing a possible (b5) by Old Maestro.

17...Ndb4

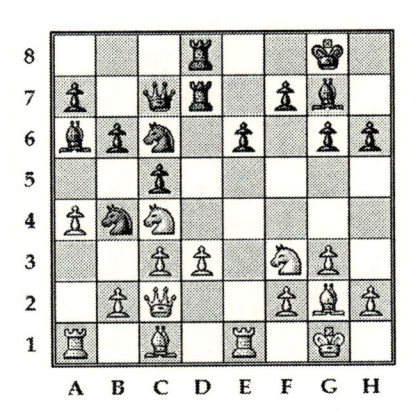

Yes, a stunning positional sacrifice by Old Maestro playing the black pieces.

18.cxb4 Nxb4 19.Qb1

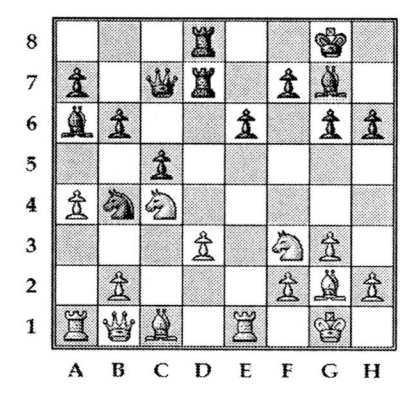

If The Great Pawn Hunter, playing white, moved his queen to e2 he would still be able to offer a fight.

19...Nxd3 20.Ne3 Nxe1 21.Nxe1 Rd1

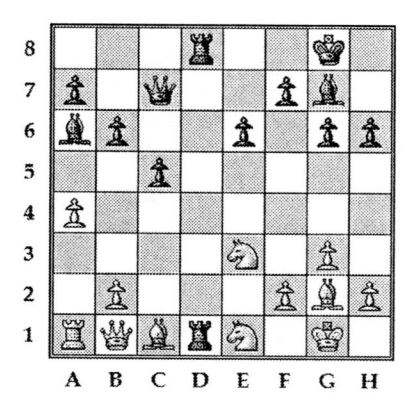

Sacrificing the exchange to get a rook on the eight rank!

22.Nxd1 Rxd1 23.Qe4 Qe5!

The Great Pawn Hunter - 255

The Great Pawn Hunter resigns for Old Maestro, playing black, has two pawn majorities. Once Old Maestro captures back the knight, all Old Maestro has to do is trade down the pieces to a won ending.
0-1

They arrived at the park and all of them went their separate ways to seek their own curiosities. The Bad Bishop was first. He arrived at the elephant's area with his bag of peanuts joyfully in hand and his sweater under his arm. He put one peanut into his left palm and said to the elephant "Here is a peanut for you elephant. Come over here." Well, the elephant just stuck his nose up into the air as if to say, "Are you kidding me, one lousy peanut. I'm worth more!" The Bad Bishop soon got the hint and offered the elephant two peanuts. "Now," thought the elephant "he will have to do better than that if he wants my attention." With no action from the elephant in sight, The Bad Bishop made the staggering offer of three peanuts. The elephant said to himself "Oh, very well, an elephant has to eat." So, he came over to The Bad Bishop and let out a mighty elephant sound, which in elephant talk means "Thanks for the peanuts." However, this elephant was more than a little chilly. It decided The Bad Bishop's sweater would complete the deal. It grabbed the last offered peanut and with one swipe of its trunk committed what in elephant circles is the equivalent of a five fingered discount. He snatched the sweater away! The Bad Bishop begged the elephant to give it back. "Please Mr. Elephant. I'll offer you a dozen more peanuts if you would only give my sweater back." But, the elephant refused. He raised the sweater high in the air as if to say, "I can fit into this. I am a perfect size eight you know (tons that is)." The Bad Bishop looked into the sky at a skywriting plane high above and shouted, "Nuts!"

Now, as that was going on, The Great Pawn Hunter arrived at the swimming pool. He didn't read the sign that said "Under construction (NO ADMITTANCE!)" He walked right on by. The reason why it was under construction was because the workmen had mislabeled the depth markers on the sides of the pool. The three foot marker was labeled ten feet and the ten foot marker was labeled three feet. One would think that a diving board on the three foot end would raise an eyebrow or two. However, The Great Pawn Hunter thought to himself "Finally, a swimming pool made for me!" He went running down the board and jumped into the air landing on the end of the board, which launched him high into the air. At a maximum height and velocity he crouched into his diving position and shouted, "Cannon Ball!!" Ahhh it was glorious...that was until he hit the water and promptly sank to the bottom. Now folks, don't get anxious. He rose from its depths and when he hit the surface he was in an all together different state of

The Great Pawn Hunter - 257

mind...Panic! But, somehow, God willing, he collected himself and put his head way back further and further until he was floating on his back just like they say in the instruction manual. The only problem was he never finished the book and only knew how to float. So, there he floated on his back looking up at the plane high in the sky....

While that was happening, The Talker and The Restless Knight arrived at the go carts. The Restless Knight took the pole position, as luck would have it, and The Talker was in the third lane over. The lights turned green and off they went. The Restless Knight was in the lead. But, The Talker came up fast on the outside. He leaned his go cart into the turn. He floored the gas and cut into the lead! The Restless Knight was up for the challenge. She drafted him on the straight away and sped up. Around the bend they went when The Talker's go cart caught an edge! His cart slammed into hers sending The Restless Knight careening off the road and into the rubber tires at the side of the course!! Folks she was out of the race. She sat in her car disenchanted and looked up at the funny plane in the sky....

Now, up in the sky, Old Maestro was oblivious to all of the events below him. All he wanted to do was enjoy the view. He asked the pilot to write a word high above where eagles soar and rainbows ark. The first two letters were "K" and "I". For the next letter, the pilot let Old Maestro write. But he was as new to skywriting as a pig is to a blanket. His letter came out as a beautiful "C", which was altogether unintended!

The Great Pawn Hunter - 258

The Bad Bishop made out the letters "K I C"...Hmmm..."It must mean 'KICK'" thought The Bad Bishop. He got an idea. The elephant was near the fence so he had the elephant trainer "kick" the sweater out from under the elephant...a job well done! He got the sweater back twenty two sizes larger but none the worse for wear.

The Restless Knight read the letters and thought to herself, "Hmmm...it is a funny way to spell 'KISS'." So, as The Talker rounded the bend to lap her, she blew him a Kiss!! The Talker was caught completely by surprise and went careening off of the roadway and into the tires at the side of the road. All of a sudden she had her chance, she "KICKED" her go cart into gear and she was back racing down the speedway on her way to victory and left The Talker looking up at the sky in wonder. His butt was "kicked" by a girl....again!

Now, The Great Pawn Hunter was quickly becoming pickled in the pool when he noticed the writing in the sky "K I C" "Hmmmm," thought The Great Pawn Hunter. Slowly he started to kick with his legs, first a foot and then two. Before he knew it he was at the shallow end of the pool. He stood up and stared up at the sky above. What was going to be the next letter?

The Pilot finished writing Old Maestro's last letter "G" to spell "KICG" But, what did it mean? When the plane landed, all the chess players were brought together. Each chess player told Old Maestro their story. They wanted to know; what did the word mean. After hearing of the adventures, Old Maestro replied, "It was the 'King' of course." God bless him.

Game
Sorin,M (2318) - Rotstein,A (2544) [B30]
FRA-chT France (7.5), 06.04.2003

The aggregate
A poem

Where eagles soar
and rainbows arch
Old Maestro left
his misty mark.

There was more at play
than we mortals know
Can we follow
where God may go?

We move to and fourth
by a sun that's lit,
one foot in front
of the other.

Friends, God is nearer
than we know it.
He can be found
in the aggregate

and we

His brother
and sister
and mother.

The Great Pawn Hunter

Downwind from Checkmate

The wind gently whispered through the leafless branches of trees, now relics. No shade for human or home for bird. But there was one saving grace for this sad dreary scene. It was the dawn of spring. In the middle of these trees, stood an old majestic figure whose quiet grace could make the trees bud and the birds sing a melody. Old Maestro came here to commune and collect. However, not bottles this time. He came to collect his thoughts, here, where no one camped and even God seemed to leave undisturbed in quiet reverence for His creation.

My friends, when you get a certain amount of grace as Old Maestro, God calls you near. Old Maestro sensed the awe of his surroundings. He stood still and glanced around him as a tear rolled down his cheek. He thought to himself "Grace, you're a funny thing. You ebb and flow as a tide unending, bringing new life into your sea and casting others upon the rocky shores. Here I stand amongst the passing and I wonder, Father, how much longer till we meet." Sure haven't we all had times like this. He would have passed from this world right there and then if it weren't for The Talker, who left the gate to The Great Pawn Hunter's yard wide open, in a strange twist of fate. For you see, The Great Pawn Hunter's dog "Checkmate" was in that yard and I want to emphasize the word "was" because, being the true hound that he was "Checkmate" went out the gate, nose to the ground, in hot pursuit of a beguiling scent called freedom.
Off he went, down Mission Avenue, past The Talker's residence, where he let out a whale that shook the

house and sent The Talker running to the window. "Ahhh!" shouted The Talker, "Checkmate is off the leash again!" Now friends, the last time Checkmate was off of the leash it was winter. Checkmate was walking the chess players home from a chess tournament that day when The Talker started throwing ice balls at them. Now, if you don't know what an ice ball is, it is a snowball with an evil attitude. Picture an icicle wrapped up in a fistful of snow for a shell. Well, The Talker started throwing ice balls like there was no tomorrow. One of the ice balls hit The Great Pawn Hunter on his leash hand, setting Checkmate free! Ahhh Checkmate, that word, there is a bit of bark in it. The bite came shortly afterwards, right on The Talker's rump. Now, there were a lot of mistakes in the history of this dog. The authorities said, from that day onward, the chess players had to fence in Checkmate! ...much like the game we love so dear.

Well, that was years ago and it has been that way ever since. But, ill feelings die hard and The Talker had been plotting and planning this for months. When Checkmate passed his house, out from his gate went our villain like a jackal stocking his prey. However, Checkmate was illusive as the hound it was and managed to evade capture. Checkmate wandered up the road, turned the corner, and out of site.

Meanwhile, Old Maestro put a knee to the ground. Then he put his hand to his forehead and sat down. Soon, he lay on his back staring up at the tops of trees and, through them, the sky above. He closed his eyes ... and drifted off...

Now, The Talker was arriving home late from a long day's work of hunting Checkmate to no avail. He twisted the knob of his front door and was about to enter his house, when, his keen sense of mischief overtook him. He looked around him and saw Checkmate coming up the street. Friends, sometimes when luring checkmate you have to offer a bone and that is just what The Talker had in his hands...that along with a baseball bat that he picked up from inside his front door. "This is too easy. Vengeance is mine!" thought The Talker to himself. He ran behind a parked car, threw the bone onto the open sidewalk and waited, downwind from Checkmate, with a smile on his face and thoughts too cruel to mention.

Now friends, vengeance has a dreary smell of hatred to it and "pay back" is a naughty word. But, I refuse to believe that The Talker was that evil, even with the events before us. You must remember he is one of us, a chess player at heart. One that did not get his fair share of love from friend or foe, but I digress. In any case, our loving God proved He had gone to the dogs that day. For, when Checkmate was about to fall into the trap, the wind picked up and blew The Talker's dreary scent in Checkmate's direction. It was just long enough so that Checkmate could escape once again! Checkmate crossed the street and left The Talker behind where The Talker lay in wait long into the night...it serves him right.
Now, Checkmate took a narrow road leading into calmer waters. He wanted to commune with nature too. When Old Maestro made his peace with God above, he was greeted with licks of affection from Checkmate. You might say Old Maestro and Checkmate were good friends...for sure.

The Great Pawn Hunter - 264

I would say that is the end of the story but our story is not over for, the next day, someone whose name begins with a "T" reported there was a dog on the loose. The police arrived at The Great Pawn Hunter's house. The Restless Knight and The Great Pawn Hunter were on the front porch playing the following game of chess. The Great Pawn Hunter played white and The Restless Knight played black:

1.e4 d6 2.d4 Nf6 3.Nc3 g6 Pirc Defense

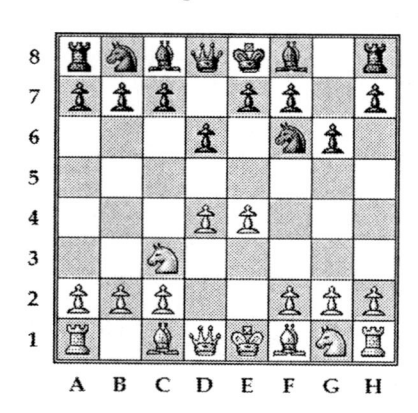

4.Be3 c6 5.Qd2

The Great Pawn Hunter - 265

The Great Pawn Hunter's white queen and bishop line up on the c1-h6 diagonal to threaten Bh6 to remove the dark squared bishop on f8.

5...b5 6.Bd3 Nbd7 7.Nf3

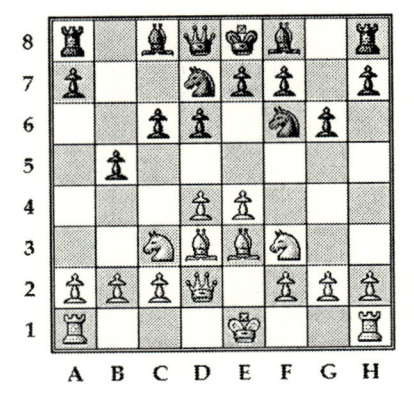

the classical center with white bishops on c4 and f4 are many times placed on d3 and e3 to fight against fianchettoed black bishops. This setup gives white many tactical attacking possibilities.

7...Qc7 8.h3

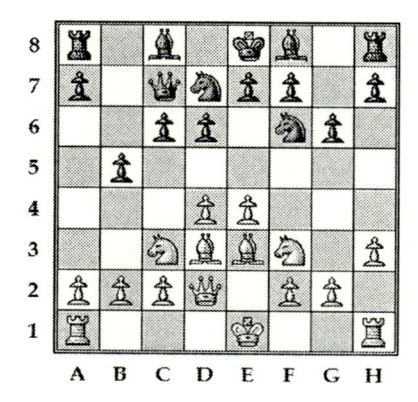

h3 keeps the black knight off of g4.

8...Bb7 9.b3

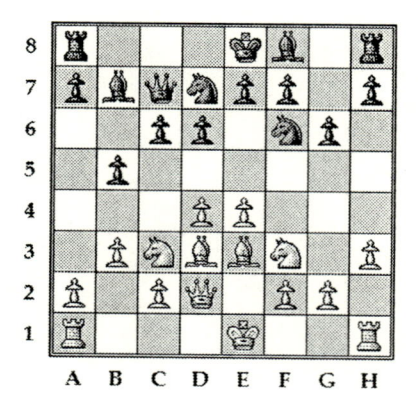

b3, although attacking The Restless Knight's outpost squares on the queen side, is a tempo wasting pawn move. When in doubt move pieces not pawns.

The Great Pawn Hunter - 267

9...Bg7 10.0-0 0-0 11.Bh6 e5 12.dxe5 dxe5 13.Bxg7 Kxg7 14.Rfd1 a6 15.a4

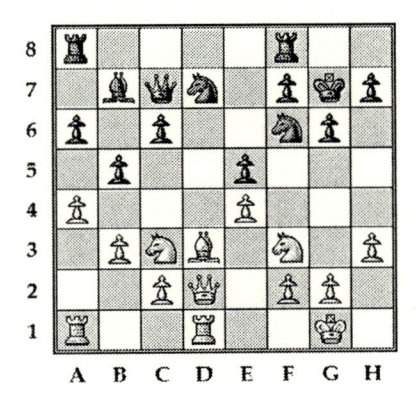

Watch the next series of moves of the d7 knight. This is a common maneuver to re-center a knight to occupy central outpost squares.

15...Nc5 16.b4 Ne6

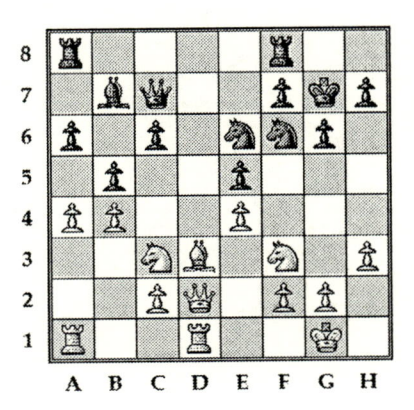

The moves a6 and eventually the double attacking move c5! will unleash an attack against the weak white e4 pawn with the bishop on b7 and the knight on f6 and at the same time attack the queen side pawn on b4, ruining The Great Pawn Hunter's queen side pawn structure.

17.Ne2 c5 18.bxc5 Nxe4 19.Bxe4 Bxe4

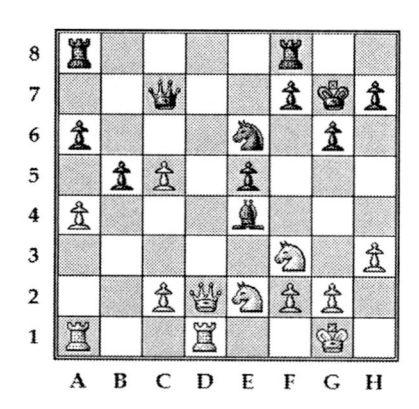

There is nothing of The Great Pawn Hunter's who is playing the white pieces to equal the powerful black bishop on e4. Restless has something tricky up her sleeves. She is going to sacrifice the bishop for the f3 knight and ruin the white kingside pawn structure as well.

20.axb5 Bxf3 21.gxf3 axb5 22.Rxa8 Rxa8 23.Qc3

The Great Pawn Hunter - 269

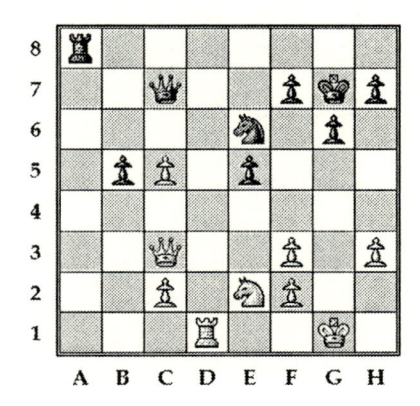

Watch how The Restless Knight activates her black rook and occupies an outpost square.

23...Ra4 24.f4 Rc4 25.Qxe5+ Qxe5 26.fxe5 Rxc2 27.Kf1

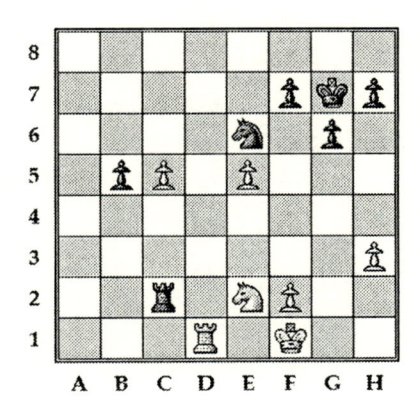

The white pawns are helpless without protection.

27...Rxc5 28.f4 Rc4 29.Kf2 Nxf4

The Great Pawn Hunter - 270

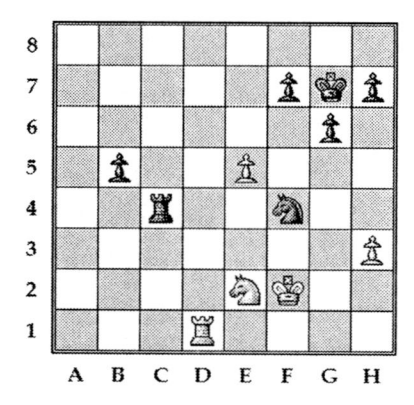

The Restless Knight playing black will trade off pieces. She will march her black pawns down the board to get a queen and the game will be in her hands. 0-1

After the game, the police entered through the open gate with The Talker close behind. They asked The Great Pawn Hunter did he see checkmate. The Great Pawn Hunter, looking at the board, responded "Sometimes. It depends on the position. It helps to think ahead. Well, really, I guess I let checkmate get out of my hands again." Ahhh, there was the evidence The Talker needed. Now, The Great Pawn Hunter was talking about chess. But, the police didn't know that. It was leaving the police no alternative but to arrest The Great Pawn Hunter for letting checkmate go.

Now, just as they were putting the cuffs on his hands and hauling his sorry self into jail, there was a sound, small at first, then louder and louder still. It was a sound of a doorknob twisting ...slowly ...slowly and then out came the old majestic one, Old Maestro, with the hound Checkmate sure to follow!

So, you say "another happy ending?" Dear friends, ...you bet!

Game
Tirard,H (2399) - Gurevich,M (2634) [B07]
FRA-chT France (4.3), 03.04.2003

The Crafty Old King
A poem

"Don't fence me in"
from the king
was his charge
to a gallant young knight
in his path very large

"I'll stand ground before you",
said the crafty old king,
buying time for his comrades
to come in from the wing.

"And I'll take off this armor
for there is no need of it.
You're young and you're weak
Me, you'll never hit."
So, he stuck out his tongue
and retracted it!

Now, this caught the knight
by surprise you could say
for the king's crazy antics
brought his men into play
and they fought off the knight
as the king hurried away
and narrowly escaped,
sure, to fight another day

And word of this story
has circled around
that tempos are fleeting
and, yes, if they're found
use them don't lose them

to keep the game sound
and use the mind wisely,
to bring the men round.

Players, checkmate's a dog
much worse, it's a hound.
and must be fenced in.
King tied up and bound.
Or, for sure he'll escape
and the trap be unwound.
The dog free as a stray
foot loose on the town.

So, take this lesson
to ear my dear friend
and your plans will be
all the more
harder to fend
and everyone looks
for a knee to bend
for you as the king
will have won in the end.

Peace and God Bless
and my love
I do send.

The Great Pawn Hunter

A Little Wee Whiskey

The night dissolved, fleeing into cracks and crevices, trying to escape the dawning light. Watching it all, The Great Pawn Hunter's grandfather sat on the top step of Eight Mission Avenue with a pipe full of tobacco, the morning paper, and a wee whiskey to warm his bones and soul as well. Now, as always, he read the chess section, which was, quite oddly enough, placed between the sports and obituaries. "Chess shares a little of both," he thought to himself. As he turned from section to section, his thoughts turned to quiet moments shared with his friend through life. The wee whiskey he placed near his side. Why? Well, you would have to know love to understand that dear friend.

Through the distance of years, ever growing with each passing day, his friendship never diminished. How could one explain the warmth of a heart, burning so brightly, it could glow eternally. He could explain for he knew. Now friend, don't shed a tear. He had his tenderness and affection through life from comforting him after a long day's work or a warm cuddle on the steps of his front porch. Well, this was all icing on the cake of a relationship that lasted through all the ups and downs. Somehow, their friendship found a way.

Players, if a friend was a flower it would be a rose with all its thorns. He had his rose and oh how the thorns of the flower do ache. What he had now, was that invisible emotion of friendship, that, and The Great Pawn Hunter. As The Great Pawn Hunter opened the screen door of his front porch, The Great

The Great Pawn Hunter - 275

Pawn Hunter glanced upon the wee whiskey by his grandfather's side. He walked to the top step of the porch and sat down with a small chess set in hand. They played the following game of chess:

1.c4 Nf6 2.Nc3 e6 3.e4 Bb4 Nimzo-Indian Defense

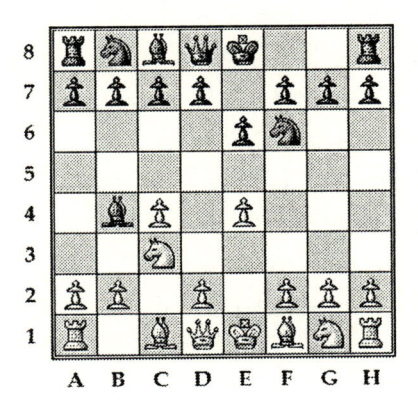

4.e5 Bxc3 5.bxc3 Ng8 6.Nf3

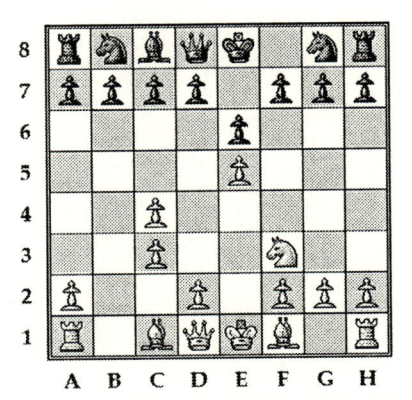

Qg4! can be very strong! This would take advantage of the absence of black's dark squared bishop on the kingside.

6...c5 7.d4 Nc6 8.Be3 b6 9.d5 Nce7 10.d6 Nf5 11.Bf4 Bb7

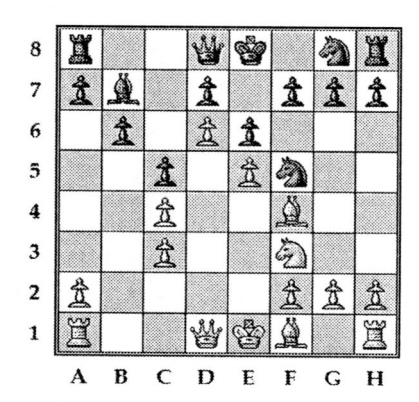

Many players are taught to advance their central pawns in what is called a "Pawn Roller." However, central pawns should also restrict the enemy's pieces. The black bishop on b7 has an open diagonal (a8-h1) and the Black knight has a beautiful central outpost on (f5).

12.Bd3 Nh4 13.0-0

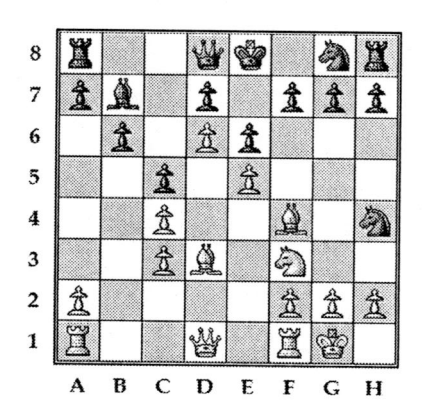

The Great Pawn Hunter - 277

Here, the black knight on h4 and black bishop on b7 team up together to break up the white pawns shielding the king.

13...Nxf3+ 14.gxf3 Qh4

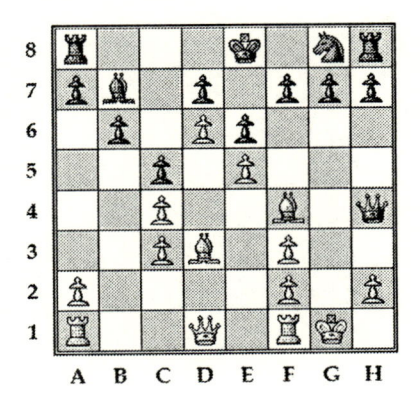

Always have a piece ready to invade when the pawns have been opened up. Here the black queen sits very active.

15.Bg3 Qh5

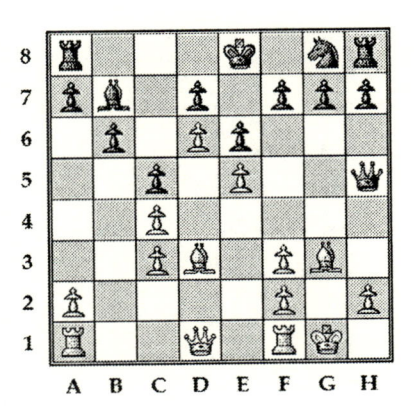

The Great Pawn Hunter - 278

It is very often true that the pawn, that has been diverted, is quite often the subject for attack as the (f3) pawn is here. Look for this in your games too.

16.Kg2 f5 17.exf6 Nxf6

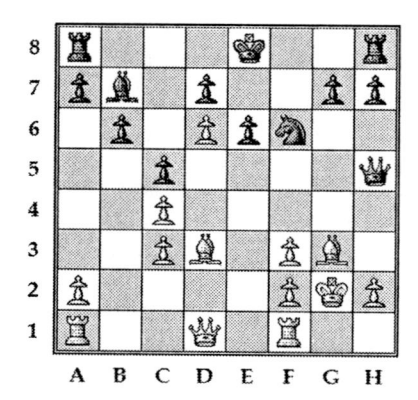

opening up the (f file) for a hostile black rook!

18.Be2 0-0 19.h4 Qg6 20.Kh3

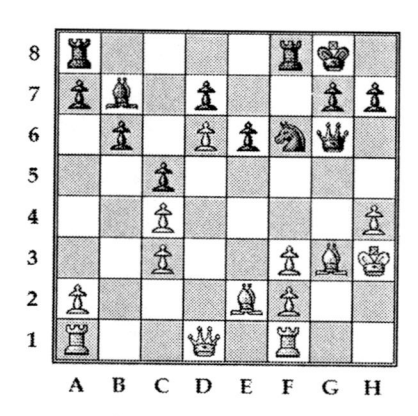

Kh3 breaks the pin of the bishop on g3.

The Great Pawn Hunter - 279

20...Qf5+ 21.Kg2 Nh5

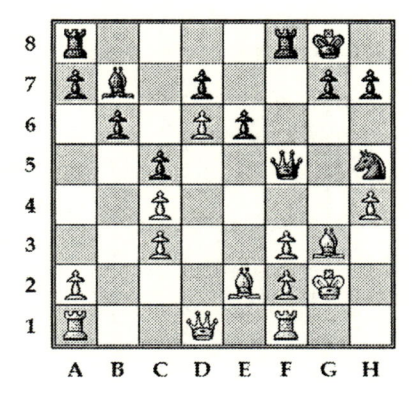

Look at all that tension on the pawn on (f3). The very pawn that was diverted from the (g2) square!

22.Kh2 Nf4!

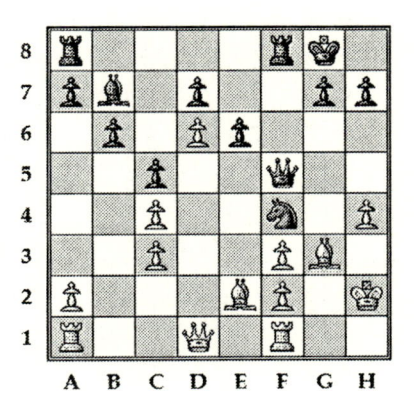

Nf4 threatens Qh3 followed by checkmate! Taking the white bishop on (g3) with the knight would only unite the white pawn structure and also bring another defender (the white rook) into the game.

23.Bxf4 Qxf4+ 24.Kg2 Rf6 25.Rg1 Qxh4 26.Kf1 Raf8

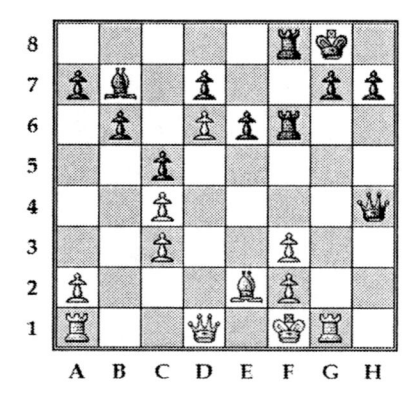

Doubling up the black rooks on the f file brings even more pressure to bear on f3.

27.Ke1

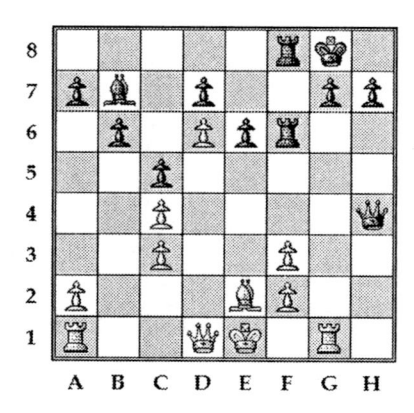

Is the white king safe? Once the remaining pawns are gone shielding the king, it will all be over.

The Great Pawn Hunter - 281

27...Bxf3 28.Bxf3 Rxf3 29.Qe2 Rxf2

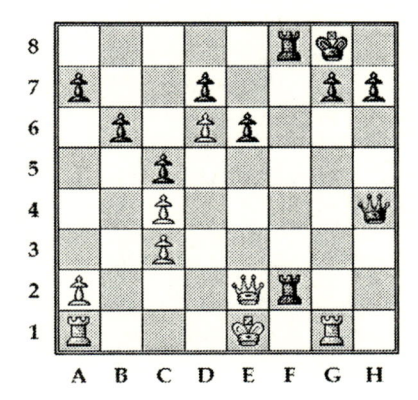

The white queen cannot move anywhere without a discovered check by the black rook on f2! [29...Rxf2 30.Qg4 Qxg4! 31.Rxg4 Rf1+ 32.Ke2 Rxa1] 0-1

"Granddad," said The Great Pawn Hunter. "Yes," replied the Grandfather. "Did you ever learn anything from that wee whiskey?" asked The Great Pawn Hunter. The Grandfather replied "Yes, son. It taught me to win half the battles!" He reached out and tenderly stroked his wee whiskey from top to bottom. For you see, "Whiskey" was the name he gave to his cat...and that my friends is the end of this tail ☺

Game
Winther,E - Malin,O [A18]
Varturnering op Vadso (2), 2000

Loom for the seed
A poem

Winning them all
does not gain one much
if they lose a friend
or a caring touch.

One can travel the world
in search of it all
with no one to catch them
...the harder the fall

The greater the distance
or number of years
can bring one to laughter
or bring one to tears.

Store up a treasure,
find peace in yourself
and you will have something
much greater than wealth.

Give and forgive
is the loom
for the seed
nurturing soil
made of many
a kind deed.

A lesson to share,
A lesson of love
may you find peace
within you
and from

God above.

The Great Pawn Hunter

Rickety Tickity Tock

The pitter patter of tiny raindrops fell on a dimly lit summer's day. As they teared down the window pane, a small figure could be seen looking out from Eight Mission Avenue. The Restless Knight looked first to the left and then to the right and finally up to the sky above...

On an old table behind her lay a chessboard. Now, this table was rickety to say the least. Held together by glue, with one leg shorter than the other, the chess players had to keep it level with a phone book on one side and their lunch plates on the other. On one side of the table was an empty chair and on the other side, in the shadows, was her friend The Great Pawn Hunter.

He was about to touch a piece and place it down on a square when he lifted his hand away from the piece. He took in a long breath of air and nervously let it out. He thought to himself, "Another move...Hmmmm...But, where is it?" Razing his eyes from the board, he looked over, to The Restless Knight, at the window. He looked down at the chessboard and let out a sigh and said, "My kingdom for a pawn," and he shook his head. He looked over to The Restless Knight at the window once more. Now, there were pawns that were at the side of the board and The Restless Knight was far away when the thought suddenly occurred to him to snatch.... (Now, now dear friends, he was not that kind of person, but it did occur to him, as temptation always does.)

The Great Pawn Hunter - 285

Well, The Restless Knight was lost in a thousand yard stare looking up at the heavens. She was no more in that room as The Great Pawn Hunter was in the game. She watched intently at the clouds...waiting for something. The Great Pawn Hunter, well, he was waiting for a good move. However, on this board, you might as well start looking for a chess oasis 'cause the moves were few and far between to say the least. He looked over once more at those lingering pawns at the side of the table...he looked...then...he looked again. Their game follows where The Restless Knight played black and The Great Pawn Hunter played white:

1.e4 c5 2.Nf3 Nc6 3.d4 cxd4 4.Nxd4 Qb6 Open Lines Sicilian Defense with Qb6.

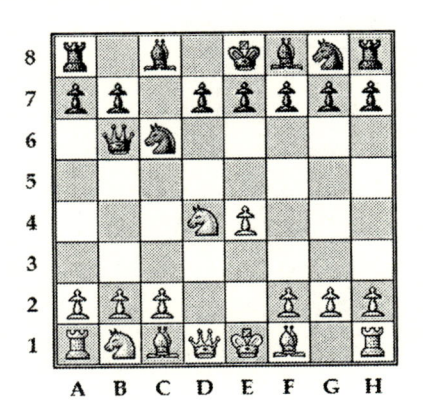

5.Nb3 Nf6 6.Nc3 e6 7.Qe2 Bb4 8.Bd2 0-0 9.a3 Be7 10.0-0-0 d5 11.exd5 Nxd5 12.Nxd5 exd5

The Great Pawn Hunter - 286

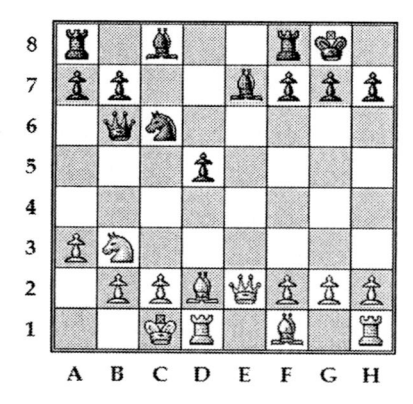

With an isolated pawn, The Restless Knight needs to attack or push it and exchange off the pawn before it becomes weak in the endgame.

13.Bc3 Be6 14.Qf3 Rac8 15.Qg3 g6 16.h4

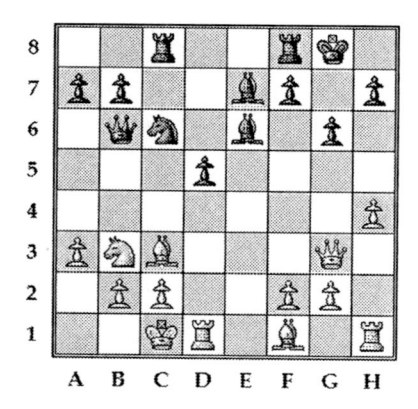

The Great Pawn Hunter playing white could have blocked the d5 pawn by occupying the d4 square with a knight. He then might look to exchange off pieces when the isolated d pawn will become weak in

The Great Pawn Hunter - 287

the endgame with no pawns on neighboring files to protect it.

16...Rfd8 17.h5 d4 18.hxg6 hxg6 19.Nxd4 Nxd4 20.Rxd4

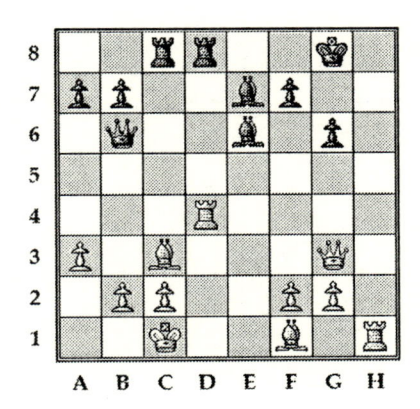

With an open h file for the The Great Pawn Hunter's menacing white rook and an open diagonal for the white c3 bishop, The Restless Knight has to do something fancy and in her mind is an "exchange sacrifice"

20...Rxc3! 21.bxc3 Rxd4 22.cxd4 Qxd4 23.c3 Qc5 24.Kd2 Bg5+

The Great Pawn Hunter - 288

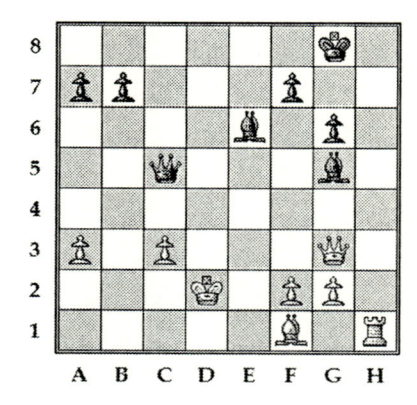

The Restless Knight's two powerful black bishops come to life. Watch and see how they overwhelm the position.

25.Kc2 Kg7 26.Bd3 Bf6

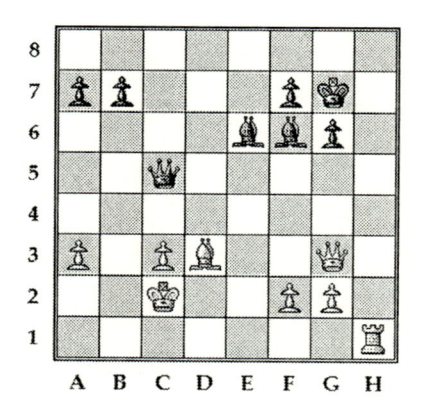

Oh if he only had a pawn on b2...This is where he looked over at the side of the board and stared at The Restless Knight's pawns!

27.Rb1 Qxc3+ 28.Kd1 Bg5 29.Ke2 Bg4+

The Great Pawn Hunter - 289

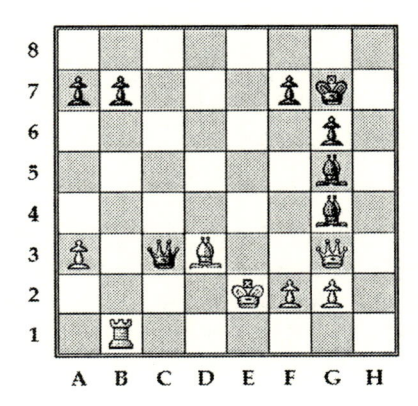

The white queen can not take the bishop because of Qd2+ capturing The Great Pawn Hunter's bishop and rook!

30.Kf1 Bf4

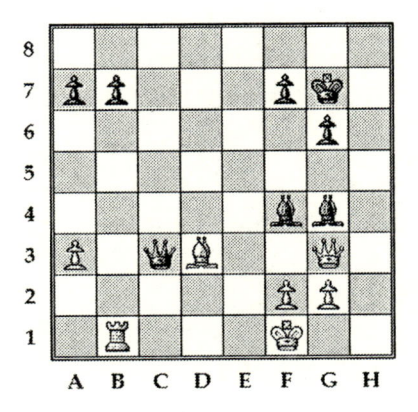

The Great Pawn Hunter just sat there with his time running on the clock, Zugzwanged by two unprotected bishops!
0-1

Now after The Restless Knight's last move, it soon became apparent that The Great Pawn Hunter's move was not going to be made any time soon. The clock ticked and ticked and The Great Pawn Hunter finally said to himself in exasperation, "Zugzwang!"

Well, The Restless Knight gazed upon those clouds and through perseverance her wish was granted. A small ray of light shone through those silver linings. She looked over at the sides of the houses. She could see the ray of light climb the clapboards of the buildings until it was just under her window and then onto the windowpane. Her eyes became radiant as the ray of light caressed the warm features of her face...she was a glow...

Meanwhile, The Great Pawn Hunter swept the whole board looking at every move. He became as unsettled as the table. He hit one of the legs of the table and the table seemed to let out a moan of its own. Did I say rickety? He picked up his sandwich to grab a bite to eat when the table lost its composure...the pieces started to slide! The Great Pawn Hunter's thoughts turned diabolical! Oh, if there where only someone there to save him!

The pieces moved onto the edges of the squares. Slowly he lifted his hand and reached ... to scratch his head. Then, looking over at The Restless Knight basking in the light, he moved his hand -- oh he would have loved to have won. But, yes folks, he placed his king on its side and joined The Restless Knight in the radiant light at the window. Restless smiled at him and said, "We gotta get a new table." The Great Pawn Hunter replied, "You can say that again" as the light rose onto his face.

Game
Motylev,A (2634) - Polgar,J (2681) [B33]
EUCup 18th Chalkidiki (7), 28.09.2002

The Servant
A poem

"Capture that piece,"
said the Knight,
"if you dare!
but don't be on edge
of that dimly lit square.
For, if the Queen
sees you laughing
and playing around,
she'll tell the King
in his court
oh so round.
And nay, say the mighty,
will know where
you're found
except in a moat
under bridge
gagged and bound."

But, the Pawn
stood ground
in his place
and did sing:

"If I take that square
alone as I am,
I am only
inviting disaster!
A Pawn is a Pawn
and a King is a King
no servant is more
than his master!"

The Great Pawn Hunter - 293

Well, the Knight
drew his sword
at the Pawn
he would slay
and the Pawn
quickly knelt
and started
to pray.
And as the sword
was sky raised,
one God,
the Pawn praised,
"no servant is more
than his master."

Now, the sky opened up
with thunder
all around
as a bolt struck
death's sword,
the Knight fell
to the ground.
And the Pawn could hear
as the Knight passed away,
words from his lips
as he weakly did say,

"God Almighty
has struck me down
by a lowly pawn
in praise!"
And the Pawn drew near
the Knight's head he raised up
as the Knight's heart beat
faster and faster
The Pawn sang to the Knight

The Great Pawn Hunter - 294

as he closed his eyes
he sang to the trees
and the clouds in the skies:

"A Pawn is a Pawn!

and a King is a King!

and no servant

is more

than his

Master!"

The Great Pawn Hunter

Trials and Tribulations

The Great Pawn Hunter sat there, across from his opponent, and in his mind he thought about the previous days events. How the police had picked him up and questioned him. "Why was he away from the house outside his curfew?," they asked. "I wanted to be with my parents." he answered. They could see he was shook up so they brought him back to his house. Today, well today everything and anything was on his mind...everything except chess! If he didn't sit on his hands and study the position he'd be picked up for loitering. You know there is a heavy penalty for loitering in this game. But, try as he could, his mind drifted off to thoughts of his parents.

The Great Pawn Hunter was playing the White pieces. Below is the position:

They were good people. They had their share of good days and bad days like everyone else in this world. His mother together with her husband, who was a common laborer, fought to keep a roof over their family's heads and now they and The Great Pawn Hunter were parted for a short time. The Great Pawn Hunter was away at chess camp. The Great Pawn Hunter was longing for them as any son longs for his parents when they are parted. "Well, when we see her again she will be washing clothes," he thought...a pun since his mom worked as a housekeeper to make ends meet. The Great Pawn Hunter smiled; so did others in the room. You see, The Great Pawn Hunter had said it aloud without thinking. Everyone thought he was talking about his opponent. Usually, his calm determined face was enough to scare the daylights out of any opponent...and now his opponent was reduced to giggles. So was he, and that was what he needed. There are few things that can change someone...faith, hope, love and chess...and with anything that is worthwhile in this world there is a struggle. That's how it was now. In his life he was struggling to cope with separation and in his game he was struggling to find a good move.

Well, the fruits of his labor were bleeding off the vine and it seemed that he would lose if only he would quit. But quitting was not his nature. Then he saw it. The weak dark squares around the Black King were too much to resist. Surely there must be a way to get at the king...and there was...

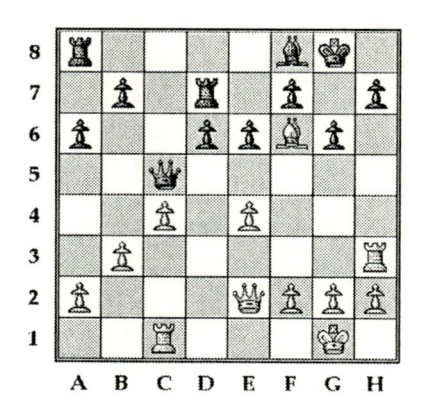

1. b4!, Qxb4

Luring the queen away from the 5th rank!

He had seen a basic checkmate "pattern" that dealt with a pawn structure similar to this. If only he could remove the pawn on (g6) it would be Morphy's mate! (with a bishop on (f6) and a rook on the (g) file.) He looked for ways to remove the pawn. He found only one. However, it would require losing his queen! Now, he was already suffering from separation. He didn't need to suffer anything else. That was bad enough. However, he remembered Old Maestro telling him a beautiful thing about the game he loved so dear. Old Maestro said "In chess, like life, You can learn to overcome obstacles."...and this had meaning for him now.

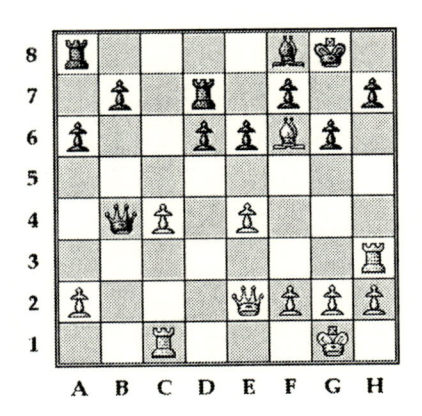

2. Qh5!

He looked deep into the position, 3 or 4 moves, and found he could play on without his queen.

The Great Pawn Hunter - 298

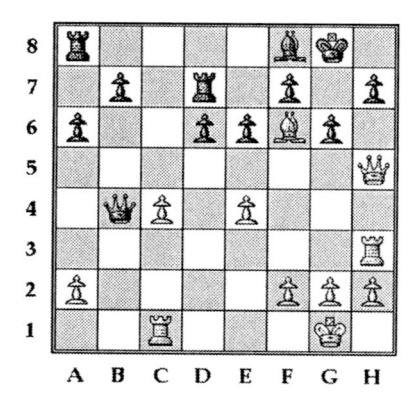

2) ..., gxh5

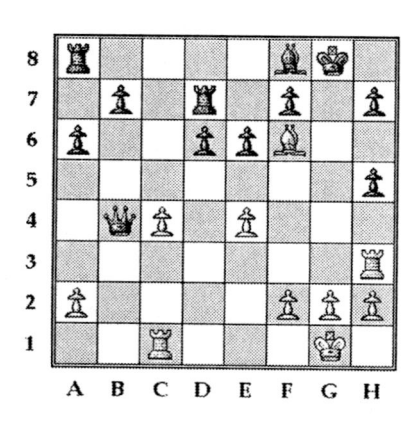

The pawn on (g6) is decoyed from protecting the king since 3. Qxh7 is mate! 2. ..., h6 is no good since 3. Qxh6, BxQ 4. RxB! and the rook will checkmate the king on the (h8) square.

Now the rook and bishop work in harmony to attack the king. The bishop sets a barrier along the (g6-h8) diagonal and the rook will attack down the (g) file.

3. Rg3+, Bg7

The Great Pawn Hunter - 299

However, his opponent didn't give up. She created an obstacle 3)..., Bg7 in a last desperate plea! ...But, this is a game. It is not real life. What do a few moves on a chessboard count for? What is a loss here or there? Why struggle? If you asked these players they would tell you..."cause it matters."

4. Rxg7+, Kf8

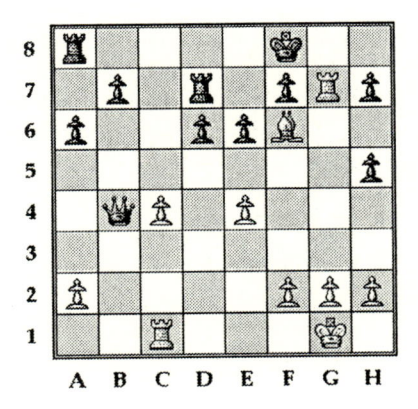

The king tries to flee to the Queenside but to no avail. The Black Monarch is hemmed in by The Great

The Great Pawn Hunter - 300

Pawn Hunter's bishop while his opponents rook on (d7) blocks his own king's escape path.

5) Rxh7, Ke8
6) Rh8++ checkmate

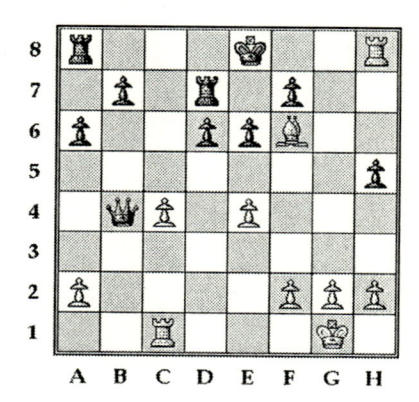

The king is checkmated by the rook on (h8).

So through a couple of decoys the rook and bishop were able to join the attack with maximum force and the king's final resting place was on his own back rank. And the queen, well, that was a part of the great scheme of things. She played her role in the chess game and his parents played theirs in life.

Game:
S. Arkhipov - S. Kuznetsov,
USSR 1980

Encouragement
A poem

When the trials and tribulations
of life beset you, as they surely will,
do not fail to meet them
in the spirit of today.

The Great Pawn Hunter's Father

Thomas Fealy
1922-2004

Openings

Alekhine's Defense 120, 195
Benko Gambit 230
Dutch Defense 185
French Defense 173, 215
King's Gambit 155
King's Indian Defense 221, 240
Nimzo-Indian Defense 275
Pirc Defense 264
Queen's Indian Defense 203
Sicilian Defense 143, 165, 251, 285
Two Knights Defense 84

Players

Alfred,N (2251) - Bogza,A (2270) [E70] 248
Bacrot,E (2653) - Lautier,J (2675) [E15] 208
Berg,E (2474) - Hector,J (2546) [C30] 160
Brossard,A (2218) - Hernandez,G (2547) 227
DEEP JUNIOR - Kasparov,G (2847) [B92] 168
Gunawan,R (2460) - Rogers,I (2475) [A58] 237
Motylev,A (2634) - Polgar,J (2681) [B33] 291
Papadopoulos,G - Ioannidis,E [B03] 199
Paschall,W (2332) - Kessler,H [C11] 177
Pavlovic,M (2500) - Roschina,T (2322) 148
S. Arkhipov - S. Kuznetsov 300
Sorin,M (2318) - Rotstein,A (2544) [B30] 259
Stohl,I (2550) - Kindermann,S (2565) [A81] ... 189
Sutovsky(GM) (2652) - C.Hansen(GM) 219
Tirard,H (2399) - Gurevich,M (2634) [B07] 271
Winther,E - Malin,O [A18] 281
Zschaebitz,K (2176) - Dworakowska,J (2350) [A80] 139

Poems

A Clown with the Blues	44
A Whale Of A Fish	178
An Angel on Top	131
An Usher at the Rectory Door	249
Bringing Down the Choir	49
Common Ground	16
Encouragement	301
Fertile Soil	190
Fighting the good fight	125
Heaven can't hold You	38
Honey From A Bee	161
Inches, Minutes, Miles	228
Inside - Out	117
Little Kitty Blues	149
Loom for the seed	282
Never No More To Weep	5
Once Upon a Center Square	91
Squirrels' Tails	209
Steam	169
The aggregate	260
The Bishop	21
The Crafty Old King	272
The Grain in the Wood	54
The King	32
The Monkey and the Bee	200
The Mountain Heights	140
The Place of Good Bread	111
The Queen	27
The Rook	10
The Servant	292
The Sleepy Sire's Ending	77

Poems - Continued

The Soap Box (e4) in the Middle 71
The Spirit Dove 220
The Stealth like Foe 96
To Catch a Butterfly 59
To Court in the Kingdom 81
To Rise and Play 63
What's In A Ring 238
Wings of a Dove 104

A

Advanced Center 196
Alternating Threats 217

B

Backward Pawn 187

C

Centralization 144
Chess Psychology 106
Clearance Sacrifice 136

D

Decoy 67, 74, 122, 196, 296
Destroying Pawn Shield 107, 156, 175, 198, 277, 280, 298
Discovered Attack 156, 281
Double Attack 61, 156, 243, 246, 267

E

Exchange Sacrifice 166, 254, 287

F

Fork 232, 246

H

Harmony 127

I

Isolated D Pawn 286

K

Knight Maneuver 267

M

Mating Net 89, 102, 123, 299

O

Opening Lines 156
Outpost 205, 242, 253

P

Pawn Center 199, 221, 241
Pawn Holes 174
Pawn Islands 268
Pawn Lever 187, 222, 267
Pawn Roller 276
Pin 87, 145, 176, 243, 245, 278
Poisoned Pawn 224
Positional Pressure 289
Positional Sacrifice 253

Q

Quartgrip 216, 218
Queen Sacrifice 231, 298

R

Removing The Defender 122, 147

S

Sacrifice 75, 86
Sacrificial Decoy 100, 137
Sealer 121
Simplification 166, 255
Spacial Advantage 173
Subtle Threats 216

Z

Zugzwang 289

Printed in the United States
57272LVS00001B/34-51